PRIVATE EYE
CONFIDENTIAL

STORIES FROM A REAL P.I.

MIKE SPENCER

11/22/19
 FoR Mark,
 Jou will know how the sausage
 is made.

99: The Press
San Francisco, CA and Lowell, MA
2017

99: The Press, P.O. Box 956, Lowell, MA 01853.

FIRST EDITION

Cover illustrated by Les Toil.
Designed by Colleen Cole.

Library of Congress Cataloging-in-Publication Data has been applied for.

ISBN: 978-0-9987204-0-1

Names and identifying details have been changed
to protect the privacy of individuals.

CONTENTS

"In the detective business, you're either a hero or a bum."
— **HAL LIPSET**, godfather of the modern P.I.

* * *

To all who have taught, challenged and encouraged me.

INTRODUCTION

MY WEIRDEST CASE occurred over a decade ago. This one was perverse enough to deserve two names, Jealous Blindman and Frozen Tampon. The story revolves around the importance of trust in relationships, with a side of porn. Or maybe it's the other way around.

For better or worse, this case was not my first connection to porn, other than as a spectator. As a reporter in Florida back in the early '90s, I replaced the reporter who broke the story about Pee-wee Herman being caught pleasuring himself at the South Trail Triple X on Tamiami Trail. The features that July night were *Nurse Nancy*, *Turn Up the Heat*, and *Catalina Five-O Tiger Shark*.

Back to the San Francisco Bay Area, ten years later. It all began with a phone call in April 2001. An old man wanted to meet with me but would not give details over the phone. He told me that his driver would chauffer him to a meeting with me at an Oakland café. Hmm, I thought, "chauffer or a driver—this could be a money-maker!" The first thing any good investigator does after the initial contact is size up the value—moneymaking potential—of each case. So, despite my suspicions, I was intrigued enough to agree to the meeting.

He and his driver picked me up at 2 p.m. in an old black town car that smelled of mothballs and vinyl. Upon arriving at Boot and Shoe Café, he told his chauffer to get lost. The two of us made our way to a back room. He lumbered along with a cane. Now I could see that he was a big guy in his 70s, looked like an ex-football player, sort of John Madden meets Boris Yeltsin. He had a shock of white hair like an excited Q-tip. It took me a while to realize he was blind. We sat down at a table and ordered coffee, and he began his story about why he needed my services.

He and his wife used to live in an upscale East Bay suburb. For years, a question had been nagging him, a question every married man wonders about at some time—had his wife appeared in a porn flick? (Okay, not every man.) As it happened, his wife was currently taking the cure at the Betty Ford Clinic and was thus out of the picture, a window of opportunity for him to hire me to look into this question. We both knew immediately that he had found the right man for the job–not because private investigator Mike Spencer's wife had in fact appeared in a porn flick, but because I would be willing to do the requisite research to get to the bottom of this quandary.

His fears were not the product of random insecurity or the dementia of an elderly man—there were rumors, and there had been an incident one day in which he had encountered some men leaving his house with 16-millimeter cameras. I quoted him a $1000 retainer, and he whipped out a wad of cash. He also provided me with a photo of his wife and some pictures of the interior of his house. My job was to scour dozens, perhaps hundreds, of porn movies to see if I could spot the moonlighting wife. Of course, the big challenge of the case was determining the possible date when the porn movie starring his wife might have played. By a strange twist, he narrowed it to October 1983: some of his coworkers had claimed to have seen the man's wife in a porno film at a specific theater— the legendary Pussy Cat in Oakland, which had stood on the corner of Claremont and Telegraph until it closed after the 1989 earthquake.

I had my work cut out for me. How was I going to determine what movies were playing at a porno house 18 years ago? I needed a crack research staff who 1) had experience watching porn and 2) would not be turned off by the hours of repetitive plot lines. Thankfully, I had such personnel at my disposal: my rugby teammates. My friend Sideshow didn't have a job at the time, so down to the Oakland Library he went to read *The Oakland Tribune* on microfiche for ads for what was playing at the Pussycat in October 1983. We were able to narrow the selection to *Anal Housewives, Pretty Peaches, Star Virgins, Up And Coming, Taxi Girls, Eruption, Spankenstein, Ass of The Mohicans, Ball Busters,* and *Night of the Spanish Fly.*

But where to obtain these "classics"? I posted notice for a reward on the rugby team's listserv. Rugger Alex duly took charge of that within 45 minutes. As if by magic, I had my VHS evidence before me, and all that remained was to watch hour after hour of questionably produced porn, hoping to find the pale, red-headed woman with many freckles on her back. My client's wife, allegedly. Naturally, I found myself facing many questions. Was this really his wife? Could it have been his daughter?

Could his coworkers be punking him? Was I really getting paid $1,000 to watch porn?

After viewing each movie about eight times, I could not find any woman matching the description. Likewise I did not see any trace of my client's house. I felt pretty sure that his wife was not in a '70s porn movie, at least not in one of the features playing at the Pussycat in October 1983. Could they have been wrong about the month? Would I have to watch all films shown in November? September? December? August? Surprisingly, I could not bear to watch any more porn. I feared a black hole of porn and disappointment. I billed for about three viewings each. I kept the movies.

I reported the negative findings, but my client wasn't *satisfied*. Something else had bothered him all these years, almost his entire adult life—he wanted to know whether his daughter, then in her 30s, was his. He wanted to meet with me again and wanted to know whether I could do DNA testing. Needless to say, I was beginning to wonder about my client. But I am an investigator—and a professional who bills by the hour. I made some calls and found a lab in Kansas that could handle such a request.

Ever watch *CSI* or another one of those true crime shows where they follow a suspect around and grab some DNA for testing? What do they use for evidence? A cigarette butt, a hairbrush, a toothbrush, or maybe even an apple core. Something normal if a little gross. That was what I was expecting. But, clearly, I underestimated my client. A couple of days later, he knocked unexpectedly at the door of my apartment, across from a synagogue near the 580 freeway. He had my address from the time he had picked me up for our initial meeting. He carried a brown lunch bag. "What's in there?" I asked nervously. "It's my daughter's tampon. I picked it out of the garbage and froze it to save it," he said.

"What? Really? A tampon? When did you get it? How do you know it is hers? Whose might it really be? No hairbrush? Really, a tampon? No toothbrush? I guess if you are paying I'm not going to bail out now, am I?"

Suffice it to say, I was now the proud guardian of a frozen tampon. I had the DNA kit so all that was left for me to do was take a swab from the inside of his cheek, bundle it up with the frozen tampon and send it off to the lab. Two weeks later we had our results. The DNA from the cheek swab and the tampon matched. He was the biological father. I called to give him the good news, but he still wasn't satisfied and wanted one more thing.

His wife was still away at Betty Ford but would be coming back to live in their home out in the country. After all my work to determine that his wife was not in porn and his daughter was his, he still didn't trust his wife.

He wanted me to bug the phones in their house to listen to the phone calls she would be making when she got home. So off I drove to the country to do this one last task. On the way, I stopped off at a Radio Shack for a small tape recorder and some phone cords and outlets. My old boss John Nazarian had shown me how to do a primitive phone bug. All I had to find was an unused phone jack in the house and install the tape recorder to a phone plug. When a phone elsewhere in the house was picked up, the tape recorder would capture the conversation.

His ranch-style house was immense and had a closet with a phone jack, the perfect place for installing the system. I finished up and went back to talk with the client, telling him that the retainer was used up and there was not much more I could do for him. He was sobbing that he still didn't trust his wife after nearly 40 years of marriage.

I left him alone in that big country house, in tears.

* * *

Not all of my cases are like this. In fact most of them can be downright dull—a private investigator spends hours sitting in a car waiting for something to happen, writing reports or checking background information on a computer, fielding phone calls from potential clients that often end up unsatisfying on both ends. But at the same time, I love my job.

I became a licensed private investigator in California 20 years ago, because it best fit the combination of the qualities I have—curiosity, tenacity, smarts—and what I wanted from my life—some control and, yes, excitement.

I want you to know about this fascinating world. My book aims to give the truth about what it means to be a private investigator. If we met at a party, and you asked me what I do for a living, I would plop this nifty book in your hand. A book can explain these things better than I ever could in a casual conversation, and it fills a void in literature, media, and pop culture about the true life of private investigations.

Right now, there are a variety of ways that we learn about P.I.s in popular culture. For people who want to undertake private investigation on their own—not recommended, by the way—there are how-to books about private investigations claiming to teach how to do your own investigations in areas of skip tracing, surveillance, background investigations, and so on. We of course have movies and TV, from the epic *Chinatown* to the shows of my childhood, *Rockford Files* and *Simon and Simon*. And there are the news headlines that reinforce stereotypes: "Private Investigators Get Busy on Valentine's Day." (For domestic cases I have found that the first warm weather of the year in May and June drives business to the door, rather than Valentine's Day.) And finally we have reality television, especially in shows like *Cheaters*, which makes use of selective editing to present a distorted picture of the work of private investigators.

My book is not *Cheaters*. Instead, I want to convey the tone, feeling, thoughts, observations, odors, and challenges I face daily. Part of this comes from a desire to help others understand what I do. I realize that my parents, most of my family, and close friends don't know exactly what I do for work. *Private Eye Confidential* is my attempt to demystify what is a complicated and downright weird profession: I'm part freak and part small businessman, and I love the dichotomy. I will do this by telling the stories that have stayed with me from my early years as a P.I. during the dotcom era in the San Francisco Bay Area. Like the author Ben Mezrich, I am writing a book for people who might not like to read. I hope to entertain those who would never otherwise read about a private eye through insights and stories that explain this weird world.

Some stories are like snapshots instead of portraits, dispatches not lengthy narratives. The tales flow like my case files: they come in, I work them on a deadline and budget, the retainer runs dry or the lawsuit settles, and I am already onto the next case. There is not always closure, or a beginning, middle, and tidy end to these stories. It's business. I don't reflect much or get too sentimental. I handle between five and ten cases at a time all the time. To paraphrase a wise rapper: I've got my mind on my money, and my money on my mind.

Any career comes with pressure. What I like about being a private investigator is you can tell whether you won or lost. As legendary San Francisco private investigator Hal Lipset put it: "You're either a hero or a bum."

I have changed names or omitted other identifying information in this book. In some cases, where a matter of public record in court files, I have kept the real names.

CHAPTER 1

LIFE OF P.I.:
HOW AND WHY

G ROWING UP IN CONNECTICUT, I liked mischief. In grade school I tied fishing line to a wallet with a fake bill hanging out to entice people to try to pick it up. (In insurance fraud investigations this is known as "roping" and is illegal.) Just as they bent to grab the wallet, I jerked the line and watched their shock and disbelief. At home, perhaps in a moment of foreshadowing, I tried to rig walkie-talkies so that I could covertly listen to conversations. As I got older I went with a crew of high school buddies to spray-paint large penises on our home football field before a big homecoming game. We did this to try to frame the rival high school; I'm sorry, New Canaan Rams. (One friend reported hearing the vice principal swearing as he used a lawnmower to trim a particularly large cock-and-balls from midfield.) We spent some weekends looking for beer bashes or trying to buy beer in New York State, where the drinking age was lower and the scrutiny of driver's licenses lax. These trips were known as "Vista cruises" after the beer-purchasing town of Vista, New York, in nearby Westchester County. A chimp could have produced more convincing fake IDs than what we carried.

As a good student and as the youngest child, I could and did get away with a lot of shenanigans. I had the academic focus and enough positive influences in my life to give me the drive to make something of myself. I speculate that being the youngest child in a large family instilled in me a zeal for competition—perhaps the most important quality in a private investigator: refuse to lose. As a teenager, my friends nicknamed me Scrappy for my style of playing softball. I was not a slick fielder but blocked every ball hit to me at second with my body. Ouch, thud, ouch.

Scrappy describes me to a tee. Other adjectives include sarcastic, dependable, obnoxious, selfish, serious, conscientious, strident, caustic, bright, judgmental, loyal, opinionated, persistent, stubborn, kind, and brave. I'm a Gemini, and I have the sign's duality. I'm more introvert than extrovert, mustering charm as needed. I've never had much interest in politics, nor am I religious; I've always had the skeptical nature of a news reporter. The whole Santa routine seemed like a hoax, and very few Biblical stories added up. Plagues of frogs? Animals two by two hopping on a boat before a rainstorm? Immaculate Conception? Rising from the dead? I couldn't buy any of it.

I planned on becoming a hotshot journalist from the time I was about 16 years old. In some ways I have achieved that goal, and in some ways I have failed. I have no regrets, especially in light of the downfall of print journalism. A good education gave me the foundation and critical think-ing necessary for private detective work. My stubborn, inquisitive nature also helped. I traveled a rare path to make it as a private dick.

It all began in a leafy suburb on the East Coast. I grew up the young-est of seven in a middle-class Catholic family in Wilton, Fairfield County, Connecticut, about an hour from New York City. Wilton is an idyllic but dull town, full of good public schools and ambitious families. All my brothers and sisters graduated from college. My parents are consummate doers, active, cheerful, and happy in their mid-80s. Their work ethic and good hearts have rubbed off on me. Many parents in Wilton, including my father, worked for large corporations. In the Wilton schools it was automatic that you would go to college and then off to some well-re-spected career in accounting, law, academia, or medicine. Trades were looked down on in a way, and you wouldn't go to college to become a cop. My own ambitions were a little ambiguous at this point, but I did well in school, especially in writing and English. I started hanging around with a bright peer group who liked to read and write. But by the time you were 16 in Wilton, you would do almost anything to escape the suffocating suburb.

When I wasn't out being a low-grade delinquent, I delivered the local daily newspaper for five years and started covering high school sports for the local weekly, The *Wilton Bulletin*. Delivering the paper introduced me to a cornerstone of small business: customer relations and collections.

Sports reporting gave me my start in interviewing people and taught me the responsibility of meeting a deadline.

I have also benefited from my experience on the high school wrestling team. The first two years I got my ass beat at meets and suffered at the hands of upperclassmen from my own team (I believe it's now known as hazing). I improved in my junior and senior years, and along the way wrestling taught me discipline and preparation, patience and the value of paying dues. It's a balancing act to try to make weight, starve yourself, practice three hours a day, and keep up your grades. Wrestling either instilled stubbornness and toughness or brought it out in me. As a private investigator I did have to wrestle my way out of a situation once—more on that later. Later in life I played rugby for fun and for anger management, but four broken bones, nine emergency room visits, and the onset of middle age ended the game for me. Recreation now means sweater vests and golf or three-on-three basketball.

I personalize some investigation work as I would have done for grappling or for a rugby match. I psyche myself up for assignments as if they were sporting events. I still get butterflies before tough jobs as I did before kick-off on the rugby pitch. It's a jock mentality, but these old habits have helped. As in sport, if I don't prepare well for a job I will be humiliated. I remember the sting of my losses a lot more than the joy of the wins. I expect victory. (I'm still pissed about losing to Duncan Morris of New Canaan High School when I lost my upset bid on a reversal with 30 seconds left in our clash at 140 pounds.)

When I entered college, I didn't know what a private investigator was or did, and wouldn't even have considered it for a career—I was too much of a snob. I picked Franklin and Marshall College in Lancaster, Pennsylvania, known for strong liberal arts. I graduated with a degree in English: I wanted academic credentials and not an undergraduate degree in journalism. Still, I kept up with my reporting, working for a local newspaper and taking a semester of journalism in Washington, D.C. After college I worked various jobs as a stringer and freelance reporter, eventually taking a job in rural Staunton, Virginia, for a year at a daily newspaper. My first big scoop was a story about a local poultry plant where machinery had maimed and disfigured several employees. I came to hear about the incidents thanks to cultivating contact with a local Occupational Safety and Health office. I got in trouble doing a Christmas shopping article that touted smaller business over a nearby mall, which happened to be a prominent advertiser in the very paper I was writing for. In other words, my early newspaper work was more community journalism than investigative in nature, but it whetted my appetite for more, and eventually sent me on my way to a full-time journalism career.

CHAPTER 2

FROM SCOOP TO SNOOP

N THE DARK I watched the silhouette of a gunman with two rifles pacing around Henry's Bar, in Berkeley, California, where he held 33 people hostage. Just moments before, I had interviewed several of the students who fled when the man opened up a briefcase, pulled out the guns and started shooting. Some of them had bloodied clothes. One witness told me how he had faked being wounded to the let the man release him and his girlfriend. (It was his girlfriend who had actually been shot and wounded, but he had her blood on him.) Henry's is right next to the University of California campus. I learned about the chaos back in my apartment while listening to the campus radio station KALX and drove up to check out the scene. (Had Twitter existed back then, I wouldn't have had my scoop.)

I found a spot in the grass across the street from the bar. Berkeley Police hostage negotiators arrived, but I was already inside the perimeter and just stayed out of the way and anonymous—just as I do on surveillance. In my reporter's slim notebook I jotted a mark for each shot the gunman fired. I counted more than 20. I was an intern then at the *Contra Costa Times* in suburban Walnut Creek and found a pay phone to call the night assistant city editor just before deadline, who in turn alerted the managing editor, who sent out a more veteran police reporter to join me. Many of the college kids in the bar, including the lone fatality, were from the paper's circulation area over the hill from Berkeley. I would later learn that the gunman, Mehrdad Dashti, was having a psychotic episode, sexually assaulting female captives, and demanding that the San Francisco police chief appear on TV nude below the waist.

I could see the black-clad SWAT team members readying themselves just before dawn. I still crouched in my hiding spot behind the perimeter. Grenades exploded, police jumped in through the bar's windows, and a hail of police bullets flew. Hostages ran, none of them shot or injured in the rescue. Minutes later the body of Dashti came out on a police stretcher, full of at least 20 holes and bleeding everywhere. In a lightning raid the SWAT team had used flash grenades to distract the gunman and free the hostages. While it was a tragedy—a man had died that night—it was also the coolest thing I had ever seen.

After a bit more reporting I drove to the newsroom to dash off a couple articles about the scene. The managing editor congratulated me in front of the newsroom by giving me a $500 bonus on the spot. I loved every minute of it.

My covering the hostage situation and shootings resulted, in part, from craving a bigger audience for my reporting than I had found at all the other smaller papers where I had worked. I had visited San Francisco after graduating from college and thought how cool it would be to go to U.C. Berkeley for graduate school. Berkeley, with its history of free speech and protests, was about as different from Wilton and the rest of East Coast suburbia as you could get. On my third try, the Graduate School of Journalism at UC Berkeley accepted me. While I had offers in the meantime from other top programs at Missouri, Northwestern, and North Carolina, there was something appealing about heading west. And, of course, it annoyed me when Berkeley kept rejecting me. I had heard that the program preferred more Ivy League candidates at the expense of those who really wanted to work as reporters. Finally accepted, I said goodbye to my girlfriend and parents and moved to the Bay Area. During the drive west, I woke up in my car one foggy morning at a truck stop in Tennessee and wondered why the hell I had left everything for the unknown. But in many ways graduate school seemed easier and more enjoyable than college, because I would be studying something I wanted and because I was paying for it.

At Berkeley, I had great classroom instruction while I continued to work in the field, first at Bay City News Service and then the daily *Contra Costa Times*. During the two-year program, I became practiced and more sophisticated at interviewing people while meeting tighter and tighter deadlines. In particular, I liked police and crime news. In many ways, journalism is great preparation for being a private investigator. Newspaper work teaches you to collect, organize, and disseminate facts with precision. And you'd better be accurate—in this line of work, there are few feelings more humbling than writing a correction for your own article.

Other big stories I covered were the 1989 Loma Prieta earthquake in San Francisco, and the 1991 Oakland Hills Wildfire that destroyed more than 3,000 homes in about 24 hours. I literally ran for my life following a fire crew on my motorcycle. Flames burst over our heads from a fire burning up the hill. Firefighters screamed at me to run, so I ditched my motorcycle and found it with a scorched seat three days later. Working as a reporter meant there was no time for shyness or hanging back when I interviewed people; I would need the same skills to canvass for witnesses as a private eye.

The discipline of tracking down witnesses in a case was learned from the practice of finding witnesses for stories. For my thesis I picked what seemed to be a story that never would have warranted more than the four column inches it received in an obscure daily. The brief reported merely that a man had shot and killed his teenage daughter before turning the gun on himself in a murder-suicide. I had to know why. I uncovered that the man was a Vietnam veteran who had been left untreated for Post-Traumatic Stress Disorder (PTSD). I obtained his military files by filing a Freedom of Information Act request. I developed enough of a rapport with the girl's grandmother that she entrusted me with a copy of the girl's diary. I persuaded a Sacramento County judge to unseal counseling records in a criminal case involving the man. I pieced together the motive for the crime and suicide: the father was jealous and angry that his daughter had started dating an older Mexican man. Information also surfaced that the father might have sexually abused his daughter. While this was part of my work, it also seemed outside of it in some way; I was finding out information that no one else had even considered worth looking for. Little did I know that the research, intuition, skepticism, and curiosity nurtured for my graduate thesis would also lead me to my ultimate career.

* * *

Though I had grown attached to the Bay Area, I left the *Contra Costa Times* in early 1992 for another job in Florida—the sunny place for shady people. What I learned in the next two and a half years covering police and news for the *Sarasota Herald-Tribune* opened my eyes to power dynamics, corruption, and one important fact that would serve me well down the road as an investigator—that people of all stripes and stations in life share the ability to lie.

In Florida, I had big shoes to fill. As it happens, I replaced Karen Dillon, the reporter who broke the stories about Pee-wee Herman nee Paul Reubens masturbating in the South Trail Triple XXX movie theater during a showing of *Nurse Nancy*. It was going to be hard to top that scoop, but I had to try.

Sarasota vibed schizophrenic. The demographic: wealthy New York snowbirds, cheap Canadians in the winter, German tourists on the beach in thongs and dark socks, Midwesterners too lazy to drive another two hours east to the Atlantic, working class Joes into beer-and-beach, a smattering of Mennonites, art students, spring breakers, and indigenous Rednecks. One joke goes: "Old people live in St. Petersburg. Their parents live in Sarasota." Elites in town pretended that it was the Athens of the Gulf Coast. Nice beaches. I will leave it at that.

With my right arm in a cast up to my shoulder, I tooled around on my motorcycle on the night-cop beat at the *Sarasota Herald-Tribune*. It was less than a week after I had shattered my right wrist in two places playing rugby in Savannah, Georgia, at a St. Patrick's Day tournament. I found that I could still take notes if I held my reporter's notebook in my left arm extended away from my body. I then jotted stiffly in the notebook with the pen in my casted right hand, looking like some sort of idiot mummy.

My city editor, a gruff bullying type, sought to clip my wings by taking me off my reporter's beat and putting me on light duty—answering phones and other clerical duties. *Fuck this and fuck you,* I thought about the situation and my boss. I even got a doctor's note saying that I could do my job, begged to go back to reporting, and got my wish. So I rode around town at night casted up on my motorcycle, looking for police news, or any excitement.

I did the night-cop beat from 2 p.m. to 10:30 p.m. Sunday through Thursday. I lived two blocks from a white-sand beach, swam in the mornings, listened to a scanner in my apartment, played rugby on the weekends, drank in local bars, and dated a coworker at the paper. And yet, I couldn't pull it all together and find contentment. The problem? Me. I argued with my editors and wound up on their shit lists. I lacked an ear for politics and could not find a way of getting along with managers. It was a manifestation of my stupidity and my immaturity. If I saw something wrong or saw a double standard or thought I was being treated unfairly, I spoke out about it, sometimes marching straight to upper management. To some degree, I blame my parents—they raised us to be independent. Four of seven of us are self-employed. If I had just kept my mouth shut more often and played nice, I might have had a long career as a journalist.

One Florida story, or non-story as it ultimately was not published, soured me on upper management. The events have jaded me to this day about the news business. The operative word: "business." News is a commodity that weighs who it kicks and who it protects.

It's rare that a medium-sized daily newspaper assigns any reporter to investigate something concrete. Most papers just want to fill the "newshole," the amount of space devoted for news, usually on the front page or in a local section. One day, though, a seemingly small crime story prompted two of my supervising editors to assign me to investigate someone and gave me a month to write the expose. The assignment came after a local TV news anchor and weatherman, stage name "Jim Jackson," was arrested on an old marijuana possession warrant out of Dade County. What raised eyebrows was the possession was for more than 30 pounds of weed when he and his brother-in-law got popped several years prior. Jackson and his station told reporters that he had successfully completed the terms of his probation and that the station had known about his background before they hired him. Still, for the station this was a public relations nightmare because Jackson had cultivated a golden-boy persona through his community involvement and hosting charity telethons. Jackson's station was tight with the local sheriff's department, frequently promoting the sheriff's anti-crime and anti-drug campaigns.

My editors and I got to thinking and talking about how something seemed amiss with the way an old warrant could simply appear like that. Jackson was hauled off to Miami before the authorities there discovered that the warrant had been entered into their warrants system by mistake. In Sarasota the initial attention over Jackson soon died down. Two of my editors and I smelled a rat, or at least a hypocrite.

A year or so before Jackson's mistaken warrant, I had reported about an international drug bust centered in Sarasota, known as Operation

Cuisinart, so named because one of the ringleaders had been a chef. More than 30 men from Jamaica to Florida to Canada had pleaded guilty in federal courts in a multimillion-dollar marijuana-dealing conspiracy. Crews sailed eight tons of pot from Jamaica into Sarasota and other coastal cities. The pot was then driven to the northeast to be sold. Ringleaders in Canada laundered the money through buying houses, a ski resort, and luxury cars. A crafty Sarasota Police Department detective had worked the case in tandem with Canadian and federal investigators. The investigators started with the low-level operatives and worked their way up the organizational ladder, compiling rock-solid evidence. Almost all were convicted, taking deals from 5 years to more than 15 years. One ringleader, Pierre Doyer, died in a New York federal prison of a heart attack.

Two seemingly unrelated events: a popular ABC-affiliate anchorman briefly in the news for an old pot-possession warrant, and an international marijuana smuggling case reaching a successful conclusion. My investigation would prove a connection between the two stories: Jim Jackson had played a significant part in the international smuggling case, even sailing a large load of pot from Jamaica to Sarasota County. He also had begun informing on others in the group, including his then-brother-in-law. He had continued his criminal activity after the initial pot bust.

A series of phone calls, named and unnamed sources, law enforcement document reviews, off-the-record talks with multiple law enforcement investigators, and interviews of former housemates of Jackson fleshed out my expose. The chef who inspired the Operation Cuisinart title was none other than Jackson's former brother-in-law, the one he was arrested with in Dade County in the earlier pot bust. I found him in a federal prison and arranged a phone interview. With my own eyes I saw the investigators' diagrams of the pot shipments from Jamaica, the names of crewmembers and dates of the voyages. Jim Jackson's name was among them. Most disturbingly, I learned how the case had really got started—one night the police had stopped Jackson with pot and other drugs in his car, starting his cooperation with law enforcement.

I had my investigative article in good enough shape that it was time to approach Jackson for comment. I thought the article the most ambitious and best reporting I had ever done. Maybe it was my ticket to a bigger paper and better paycheck. But the story never ran because the executive editor, a savvy political player in the community, caught wind of it and killed my project. Her reasoning boiled down to Jim Jackson's stature and popularity around town being too great to run such an article. This time I didn't fume to her or the other editors. I just sucked it up and swallowed my own bile.

After that, I had one last shot for an ambitious story. I botched it. And I can't blame editors, only myself.

Management shipped me to Siberia—or rather, to the Bradenton bureau—after I got caught lying to a murder suspect I had tried to interview in a jail in El Dorado County, California. The suspect was from Sarasota, and was accused of murdering his boss's new wife, a wealthy Sarasota woman who had just moved to California with her husband. I flew to California on my own time and money to investigate the case. The defendant and his boss, also charged in the murder, were accused of beating the woman to death in their new house and then staging a car accident in an attempt to cover up the grisly homicide. At the jail the man asked if I had permission from his attorney to speak with him. At the time, I did not know he had an attorney, and I should have checked. Instead, in a split-second decision, I lied to the defendant and told him I did have permission. Huge mistake. The man didn't tell me much in the interview, but he did tell his attorney about my lie. The attorney promptly called my bosses back at the paper in Florida to complain. It was the biggest professional sin I ever committed, and I regret it to this day. Ultimately, the defendant and his boss were both convicted of the murder and are serving life sentences in prison.

In the Bradenton doghouse, I could only take so much scribbling about weather, parades, and community affairs. I had been neutered. A couple months later a friend from journalism school told me she was leaving her apartment in Berkeley and asked if I wanted it. I decided to accept and quit the paper. In October 1994 I hopped a plane to San Francisco and had my motorcycle shipped to Berkeley.

Back in California again, I did freelance journalism for about four months while looking for fulltime employment. I didn't want to go back to double- or triple-A newspapers, but there were no openings at the *San Francisco Chronicle* or *San Jose Mercury*. I ate rice and beans most days and considered selling some of my clothes. Finally I saw a help-wanted ad in *The Oakland Tribune* for something called "an AOE/COE investigator." I learned upon being hired that it stood for "arising out of employment/course of employment investigator." I had backed into becoming a private investigator.

The most common path to private investigator is as a policeman. Now I ask, why didn't I become a cop? For one thing, I don't like authority and rigid hierarchy. I used drugs in college and didn't feel like lying about it to pass the application. I have poor eyesight. I am not comfortable around guns. I gravitate more towards underdogs and helping to defend people. I was once arrested for auto theft in college, though I thought of it as technically a joy ride and the case was expunged. In a lot of ways I was not prime law enforcement material. But I respect the good officers and detectives who protect us and deal with horrific situations every day.

I still wonder about another potential investigative path—why did I not become a lawyer? The main reason is that I associate being an attorney with being chained to a desk. I like fieldwork, fresh air, and a lot of variety. There's too much stuffiness in the legal world. In photos, do members of the Supreme Court ever look healthy or like they are having fun? They look embalmed.

I soon learned the differences between journalism and private investigations. While the process might be similar—both involve research and writing—the end goal is different. In journalism you strive to publish your work and crow about it. In investigations, you show your work to your client alone and keep your mouth shut. Journalism pays you for your discovery, while private clients pay you for discretion and problem-solving. Journalism is collaborative and fairly social; private investigations are often solitary and isolating.

Journalism also helped build my bullshit detector. The experience taught me that most people have an ax to grind and that most people withhold information. Newspaper work also introduced me to many decent people who, while simply trying to do their jobs, due to horrific events became public figures or witnesses. You need both skepticism and a big heart for both reporting and investigating.

CHAPTER 3

THE DAILY BUSINESS

"DON'T YOU REALIZE everyone in the world is at work and at a job at nine in the morning?" a college professor once growled as I groveled to explain why I had missed his class on the day I was due to give a crucial presentation. I had overslept that morning in my junior year, despite going with a two-alarm clock system. By then, I had become a diligent student who didn't party too much during the week and who prepared well. My mea culpa worked; he let me give my presentation late and gave me a B or B+ in his upper-level class.

I bring up this crusty professor because I have created a schedule for myself where I don't always have to be at work at 9 a.m. I do however follow a normal routine, unless surveillance or a difficult service of process is on the docket. A normal day starts at 7:05 a.m. with my iPhone alarm set either to Los Straitjackets' cover of Los Bravos classic "Black is Black" or to Ozzy Osbourne's "Crazy Train."

On most days by 8 a.m., Daisy Dog, staff canine agent, has scarfed her breakfast from the automatic feeder and needs her morning exercise to keep her Labrador fighting weight of 72 pounds. I go for coffee with her and then head to find a trail or a local park for her to chase and retrieve some wedge shots. It doesn't matter if it's pissing down rain, dog has her romp, and I need to get out of the house. Dog and I are tight. She hears my interviews and statements over the phone in the home office. She has proved vital in a few pretext investigations, door knocks, and service of process. There's nothing better than a dog in a suburban neighborhood to allow you to get close to a house. Because I work from home, I need that separation in the morning before I return to the cave to begin work.

Some mornings I go for a jog and hit the pull-ups and dips or do a couple weight exercises at the gym. I can't shake the concern that I will need to use my brawn on the job, but really my brain drives the business.

Still, I engage in mental tasks quicker and more effectively after a work-out.

Until I bought my house and got married 11 years ago, I would rent an apartment but also rent an office. I liked having offices around down-town Oakland but the biggest added expense was parking tickets. Many times on this job you have to bolt on a moment's notice, so parking all day in a garage is not realistic. For now I have a good working solution: I use a virtual office in Walnut Creek, a tony East Bay suburb, if I need office space to work without distraction or a nice place to meet potential clients. Someday I might very well have another brick-and-mortar office, but for now paying a big mortgage and a pricey office rent does not make sense.

On a less typical day, I might finish the day by meeting an attorney and a witness at crime scene, in order to prepare for trial and decide ex-actly what the witness will say. If the crime occurred at night, I will visit the scene at about the time of night the crime occurred in order to expe-rience the lighting conditions and other details that could have affected what witnesses or police saw. Any good attorney or investigator knows you have to inspect the scene.

One week in June on a Tuesday and Wednesday I conducted 22 hours of surveillance over an afternoon and into a brutal second day. I was in-vestigating whether an expert witness from out of town had arrived far in advance of a deposition and sure enough, at the end of the surveillance, there he was. There is nothing more disruptive to a smooth work pattern than a balls-out surveillance detail. You can't get any other work done because surveillance demands all your focus and energy. But at $125 an hour it's a good chunk of coin and worth some fatigue.

There is a price to be paid for a weird work schedule and hours, and this is something I have really learned only in the last year or two. My critical hours for reaching witnesses tend to be Monday through Thursday from about 5 to 7:30 p.m. and Saturdays from about 10 a.m. to 1 p.m. At one time I helped coach a local high school rugby club, but practices were in the evenings and games were on Saturdays. I withdrew from coaching because if I couldn't fully commit to the team, I would be doing them a disservice. By the same token, I was also not realizing my business potential and by not making myself available to clients during these critical interview hours. (If I apply myself, the corporation should gross about $120,000 this year. Of course, the numerous unpredictable expenses mean that I can't be sure on what the net income will be.)

My biggest complaint about working as a private dick is the solitary lifestyle; the opposite of working in a newsroom. I've always liked being part of a team. I've played team sports since I was eight years old. I like the concept of a common cause and teamwork. Sure, I have work associates and clients and a partner, but we seldom work together on a daily basis. But maybe this is just the way it is for many professions in the brave new freelance economy.

Now that I've been a private investigator for longer than the run of *Cheaters*, I know the priorities. Almost every week I make a big list of my ongoing cases. From that I have a loose matrix of which case gets highest attention. No surprise that I go with the most regular clients first. They have been with me longest, give me the most work, and pay on time. They are gold. Without them business would take a big hit. Next would be the hottest of the "one-hit wonders." Sometimes I get a new large case, especially thanks to the Internet. The challenge with private clients is to honor their requests and do a great job because it's likely the only time they have ever used a P.I.

Much of my success depends on my marriage, and I don't mean that in the "Stand by Your Man" type of way. I am married to a wonderful, hard-working woman who runs a skilled nursing facility. We don't have kids. We are also deeply committed to our respective work. We have different schedules and lifestyles, but we make it work. During the week she is not around that much, enabling me to work very odd hours if necessary. I have told her that while I would love for her to come work for me, we would either become highly successful or kill each other. She is entirely smart, organized, and business savvy—and she even recorded my business voicemail message. It's just that we have different approaches, which aren't entirely compatible. We both like helping clients and solving problems, but she likes a regular schedule, while I need to mix it up. She's planning for an early retirement, while I can't imagine life without P.I. work. Whereas my wife manages people and depends on colleagues and coworkers every day, I have little to do with my P.I. peers. We work together here and there or trade information and sources, but it's not a close relationship. I don't fraternize or socialize much with fellow private investigators. It seems that when we gather at conferences or functions it usually devolves into one-upmanship and bragging about one's own greatness or how much money was made off a client.

What do I think of my colleagues? Some are incredibly brilliant, polished, educated, hard-working, sharp people. Some are knuckle-dragging mouth breathers who never change their pants. Some are rip-off artists. Many lack social skills, which hurts when you need to cultivate witnesses and interact with a range of sources and bureaucrats. I have now personally known a total of five private investigators and information brokers who have been sentenced to prison for breaking laws on the job. What they have in common is that they couldn't resist easy money. Their offenses ranged from hacking computers and emails to illegally obtaining phone records. Before I take a case, I always step back to consider the assignment, the client's character, and the odds of success in handling the case with above-board methods.

I know there are at least a few among my private investigator colleagues who have previously been forced out of law enforcement due to scandals when they wore the badge. There are rumors, but I'm never sure whether these ex-cops committed crimes or just had lapses of judgment. Whenever I read an article about some police dust-up or disciplinary action I think to myself, "Great, here comes more competition." I can be a petty bastard at times, but I don't like more sleaze in my profession. Or maybe I should welcome a dodgy P.I. because he will just make me look better by comparison?

A decent personality is a big plus in the private sector, where you are either selling your services or selling your trustworthiness to a witness. It helps if you can talk to anyone. Women have a big advantage in the field. Why? They are perceived as less threatening, and most are adept listeners. As investigators a central component of what we are doing is selling ourselves. If I don't get witnesses talking, I am not doing my job. I don't know if what I have is charm exactly, but maybe in my approach there is some sincerity with a hint of desperation that appeals to people.

I have noticed that private investigators like to call themselves "groups," as in The Mintz Group or Diligentia Group. The other common practice in naming a business is to add "and Associates" to the title, as in my former employer Maxwell and Associates. Those names are fine, I guess, although "group" strikes me as slightly pretentious. I named our company "services" with the intention of protecting a client's anonymity: if the invoice comes to accounting, the business name would not provoke unwanted scrutiny. Euphemistically, "services" could include anything just short of assassination, I suppose. Some businesses go for obscure, cinematic titles: Thin Blue Line, Special Circumstances, Third Echelon, etc. My favorites include Sunrise Investigations and Know It All. "It's a fine line between clever and stupid," to quote a band member of Spinal Tap.

P.I.s tend to use embarrassing email handles including lots of 007s, Magnums, Sherlocks, and the like. I hate the magnifying glass, Maltese falcon, and fingerprint images used all too frequently in P.I. ads. Yet, I have used my schlocky email "Hirepimike" for far too long. And what else says uber dork like my Hall and Oates "Private Eyes" ringtone?

Regardless of corny business naming practices, the job always comes down to results. The skill-set for quality investigators includes closely reading texts and documents—and not all P.I.'s sweat the details. The abundant reading and studying I did as a kid and in higher education pays off. I have a plodding and deliberate way of working. In personality assessments, I would be deemed a "pacer" as opposed to the "doer" or "talker" who go 100 miles per hour all the time. The downside to my caution is that maybe I'm a little slow; the upside is that I rarely make mistakes.

In many regards, a private investigator is a lot like any contractor, plumber, painter, or tradesperson. Most of us have our niche or book of business. For me, those would be the lawyers who provide most of my business. An advantage of having been in the business a while is that I can quickly figure out who the good clients are and who will pay fast or at least on time to keep my cash flowing. When you are starting out or early in your practice you tend to take Anything For a Buck, but you do not want to be a long-term member of AFAB. So, lawyers fill most of my dance card, and private clients make up the remainder. When I am busy and humming on all cylinders, I require a big retainer to take on a new client, especially a private one.

I follow a mental checklist to determine whether I take a case from a private client, or any client really. Factor one? Let's be honest: cash. For a private client I want a retainer of at least $1500 if it's going to involve surveillance or more than 10 to 12 hours of work. Straight up: nothing is worse than chasing people for money. (I turned down a job doing court-appointed criminal defense investigations for the Alameda County Bar Association over cash-flow issues. The program paid $50 an hour, too low for my liking, and was reportedly taking 60 days and beyond to pay. Low pay plus slow pay equals business killer.) I love criminal defense cases, but I have no pension while I'm balancing a mortgage on a nice house, household and business bills, green's fees, and a Labrador who likes to live in style.

I try to plan my work and daily schedule, but the job is fluid. I have to leave room for chaos. As Mike Tyson put it: "Everybody has a plan until they get punched in the mouth."

CHAPTER 4

"ARE YOU LIKE THAT SHOW *CHEATERS*?"

O N A SLOW, sunny Sunday afternoon in San Francisco I leaned up against a railing above Sacramento Street. I had *her* car, parked down below, in my view. I carried a Pentax camera with a mirror lens, sort of a compact telephoto. My job that day was to follow a client's cheating husband. So far I had seen him together with his lover, before losing them on the surveillance. I had nothing to do but stake out her car and pray I got a compromising shot of them together if he dropped her at her car. (Being a good surveillance op always means anticipating the next step.)

I was right. Lover Boy dropped her at her convertible, then leaned in for a big, long, sloppy goodbye kiss and grope. Click, click, click. She drove away. Now I had the photos, but I still had to follow her to learn her identity. One big problem on that 1995 day: my car. I drove a 1975 baby-shit brown Dodge Dart that I had bought off a Berkeley blues guitarist for $500. In order to start the engine I had to lift the hood and connect the points with a long screwdriver. She already had a helluva head start. But I knew she was heading for the nearby Bay Bridge, or at least had a hunch—when you lose someone on a tail, if in doubt drive straight. I did, about 85 mph flying east on the Bay Bridge. I caught up with her near the Oakland side and followed her to where she lives in Hercules, about 15 miles from San Francisco. I learned she was a nurse.

I developed my film of the great kiss-grope and turned it over to the client. Someone, I assume, was in big trouble. We do get cases like these as private eyes, but I hope to dispel the impression that domestic stuff is all we do. At cocktail parties, if I slip up and mention what I do for work, I usually get asked: Do you catch the people faking injuries? Do you have to be licensed? Do you carry a gun? Are you like that show *Cheaters*?

Yes, I look for people faking injuries. Yes, in California you better be licensed. No to packing heat, but I will welcome a trusted associate or partner qualified with a gun to watch my back.

And if you haven't seen it, *Cheaters* was a syndicated reality TV show from 2000 to 2012. It featured supposedly real domestic investigations where a host and client would confront the subject of the investigation. What gave the show away as fake to me were the captions like "Investigation, day 13"—I don't have domestics that go on for 13 straight days because almost no one could afford it. *Cheaters* was like Jerry Springer filmed outdoors, truly a low point in American pop culture.

And yet...I am doing *some things* like *Cheaters*. I do chase cheating spouses. I do perform surveillance (my obsessive knowledge of Bay Area sports, National Public Radio, and local public bathrooms can tell you that). I have used pen-sized cameras. But if *Cheaters* were my life...it wouldn't be much of a life.

Although my job is a strange one (face it, you wouldn't be reading a book about a misunderstood district manager), I'm not completely alone. The California P.I. license numbers are now up into the 27000-range. My original P.I. license number is 18828, and I have not seen a P.I. number below 12000 in a long time. Keep in mind that not all licensed private investigators practice.

California has tough requirements for a license. You are required to have 6000 hours work experience, three years full-time, and pass a two-hour exam designed to weed out cowboys and goofballs. I argued that my journalism experience should count for 2000 hours and it was accepted. Most veteran ex-cops pretty much only have to sit for the test. Apparently, the fail rate for the exam is 70 percent. (I failed first time, took it again, and passed.) Many states still have very little or no licensing requirements. Rogue private investigators go to states such as Colorado, Missouri, or Florida where the scrutiny and requirements are relaxed. California, Nevada, and New York tend to have the tightest standards for licensing and regulating private detectives. (As of this writing, Alabama and Colorado just passed laws requiring that private investigators be licensed.)

The Bureau of Security and Investigative Services under the state's Department of Consumer Affairs regulates and licenses private investigators in California. The Bureau defines P.I. activity as follows: "A private investigator is an individual who (1) investigates crimes, (2) investigates the identity, business, occupation, character, etc., of a person, (3) investigates the location of lost or stolen property, (4) investigates the cause of fires, losses, accidents, damage or injury, or (5) secures evidence for use in court."

Private investigators do everything from gathering competitive intelligence for multinational corporations to tailing cheating boyfriends to finding all kinds of evidence for all kinds of lawyers. Whenever there is a dispute involving money or any kind of legal action, a private investigator will be in the picture. We are less exotic than people imagine. I sometimes joke to myself that I am more like "Mike Spencer, Freelance Claims Adjuster," but that doesn't sound so sexy.

In fact, I look for excuses sometimes to turn down cheating spouse work. I'm getting older and don't need the aggravation. But then I get the itch for another $1,500 retainer, I find myself developing a rapport with my client, I start feeling the competitive surge, and out into the night I go. Maybe the next one I will get a fat payday on a case that lasts 13 days. My highest-paying domestic was $9,000 on a case some years ago on which I subcontracted four other investigators on an extended surveillance of a client's husband for three days and nights while he was staying in a downtown Oakland hotel. We even knew his room number and the names of the people staying in adjoining rooms. Under our watch he was faithful. Still, I was paid—answering the phone can have its benefits.

Another reason I take calls on domestics: one of my surveillance associates was once hired to track a cheating husband on a 10-day cruise in Tahiti. The client paid all his expenses, plus his hourly rate. My associate put in the work to obtain evidence of the husband's infidelity, but also had a lot of downtime to enjoy the cruise. I'm still waiting for my gig in Tahiti to come along.

Another question I get: Do you read lots of detective books? No, I don't. I do appreciate crime writers such as James Ellroy and Dennis Lehane, but I don't go in for the whole mystery genre. To me, the lush, exotic settings and well-heeled private eyes and clients are the literary equivalent of the highly unrealistic Magnum P.I. My own experiences and clients are heavier on grit than intrigue or romance.

CHAPTER 5

HOW I PICK MY CASES

NOT LONG AGO, I had to serve papers on a woman involved in an auto crash. I went to her place at night, assuming what I was in for was just another routine service of legal process. Unfortunately, the door was answered by the woman's husband, a burly taxi driver from Nigeria who didn't take kindly to a stranger with bad news for his wife. He charged at me on the doorstep. I pinned his arms to his sides with a gargantuan bear hug—he might have had a knife or other weapon, and I was not going to give him any swinging distance or leverage. After a few seconds I released him and ran. I called the cops on him but nothing came of the situation. Assaulting a process server is akin to assaulting an officer of the court, though I don't think there's anything specific in the California penal code for it. I immediately raised my rates for the attorney who had given me the assignment. I learned an important lesson: be ready for anything and never let anyone get too close. My business partner Jeremy Elrod, a former Army Ranger, has accompanied me, handgun in ankle holster, on a few serves in more dangerous parts of Oakland. You can't ask for better protection than Elrod.

While I can't predict what will happen in the field—for example, being attacked by an enraged taxi driver—I try to steer my work towards profitable areas I know I can handle.

As with any small business, you have to blow your own horn. Too many private investigators expect work to just fall into their laps. I never get too complacent. I know that if I don't answer the phone, the potential client will simply call the next P.I. on the list or the screen. Still, my process of picking clients and cases has evolved over the last two decades. One of the first private investigators I ever met in San Francisco, John James Nazarian, taught me that in selecting clients and cases, the right attitude is key. Attitude doesn't mean arrogance, but recognizing that by valuing our work and the service that we provide our clients, we deserve to be paid well for fixing their problems or obtaining timely, relevant information.

Nazarian moved to Los Angeles after I worked for him in the mid-'90s. A former sheriff's deputy in San Francisco and in the Central Valley, Nazarian imparted this advice about signing up domestic clients: "Meet with them while they still have tears in their eyes." He also reminded me to never hold back in billing attorneys—after all, we help make them big money. He bills at about $450 an hour. While he is not the most highly skilled investigator with whom I have ever worked, he likely is the best marketer. His other smart move is to surround himself with good help, such as me.

Back when I was a novice investigator, I served as Nazarian's bagman, signing up clients and collecting money for him. I vividly remember a warm San Francisco night with him in his Jeep looking for witnesses in a criminal case. I had just broken my collarbone playing rugby so every jolt and bump in the Jeep hurt like hell. Nazarian didn't care. He had work and a paying attorney client to satisfy. I worked my first successful domestic through Nazarian, and we almost got in big trouble together on a murder case. He taught me that it's good to have a partner in sensitive investigations with difficult clients.

Over the years I have carved a niche working for trial attorneys, also known as consumer attorneys or by the derogatory "ambulance chasers." I also get work from criminal defense lawyers. Working for criminal defense and for plaintiffs' attorneys butters my bread. I handle a ton of vehicle collision matters, dog bites, sidewalk defects, and trip-and-falls for plaintiff's lawyers. Each incident scene needs to be documented and measured and photographed because an insurance adjuster on the other side will be doing the same thing; my prerogative is to beat them to the punch. In addition I have a whole bunch of other lawyers and paralegals who always need witnesses located, assets found, and people interviewed; sometimes they just need plain dirt.

My early years of investigating workers' compensation claims did not involve surveillance, but the questioning in the field and at workplaces taught me how to take statements. In workers' compensation investigation, I found that some of the most egregious frauds are pulled by prison guards and firefighters—when they go bad, they go rotten.

One story of public servant greed involves a state parole agent who liked his young ladies. He owned a yacht and hired ex-cons to work on it—in effect, using the criminals he was supposed to be supervising as domestic help. One day, his supervisors came to find out about the demographics of his labor pool, landing him in hot water. His response as a state employee in the face of discipline? He went out on a stress claim.

Mr. Parole Agent had planned well. Before he got in official trouble, he started taking out many credit card applications. He had a steady income and good credit; by starting out paying on the cards and increasing his limits he was able to take out about $300,000 in credit, putting a lot of money at his disposal.

His other pursuit was underage girls, especially young police interns, dating several of them at the same time. After he lost his Skelly hearing, the step that allows a public employee to argue his case before the official discipline is announced, he persuaded one cadet to run away with him to Bora Bora. With his young lady by his side and flush with cash advances on credit cards, he pulled the plug and went off sailing around the world. He figured the credit debt would go away after five or seven years. Here was a workers' comp claim that clearly deserved investigation as a possible fraud, but the state wasn't going to pursue him. I thought of him the other day and looked up his name on a state web site. I see that he landed on his feet back working for the state as, drumroll please—a supervising fraud investigator.

Some private investigators stick to specialty fields like workers' compensation and investigations for large insurance companies. I know several who handle criminal defense cases almost exclusively. Others have carved niches doing sensitive workplace investigations relating to sexual harassment, racial or age discrimination.

Still, I suppose 70 percent of P.I.s overlap on the same tasks but maybe in different arenas. Were it not for my attorney niche, I would have starved to death waiting for the phone to ring from Yellow Pages (dated reference, I know) and Internet ads hoping to hustle surveillance and cheating spouse gigs. Private investigators often fail not because they are bad at investigations, but because they are bad at business. What separates the successful private dick from the others is the same tenets of any business: results, reliability, credibility, marketing, answering the phone, returning calls and emails, and generally being on top of business.

Through experience I have become much smarter about good business practices, more tactful about dealing with potential clients, and more acutely aware of sending out invoices and collecting in a timely manner.

If about to work for a private client rather than through a lawyer, two questions I ask myself are: do I like them, and can I help them or can I/ we win? Within two minutes on the phone with a potential new client, I know whether I want to help them and work for them. I am happy to give 15 minutes of time on the phone to see if we might be a good fit for each other. And 80 percent of callers don't really know what they want. I had one recent caller who had called four or five times within the past six months after I turned her down. She let slip that some other private investigator had turned her down and, based on her inability to tell a concise story or stick to a point, I had to refuse service to her. When people want me to locate people for them or run license plates to find the name of a registered owner, I tell them the request had better be in conjunction with a documented legal case filed in a court. Why? I want to sleep at night and therefore I am not just looking to make a couple hundred bucks for turning over an address to a potential stalker or miscreant.

What gets many private eyes in trouble is a failure to manage and communicate with clients. You owe a duty to any client who has paid a retainer and signed your contract. Should you find you don't like the client, do the job to the best of your ability, provide a report and final invoice, and move onto the next one.

Yes, we do get calls from mentally ill people. It's cruel, but many P.I.s refer to this element as the tin-foil hat brigade. Many of these harbor paranoid delusions of landlords or former bosses following them, tapping their cell phones, and bugging their apartments and computers. With so much security camera stuff available online, I try to redirect them to shopping for various camera systems that they can install *themselves*.

Nonetheless, I am happy to talk with a potential client for five or ten minutes even if it doesn't lead to business. A long time ago I received a call from a woman in Alameda who was convinced her husband was sneaking mistresses into their home at night. Before taking the job, I grilled her to make sure that she wanted to hire me. I was not going to take her money casually. So, for about $1000, I sat in my Honda Accord on a quiet street in Alameda from midnight to 6 a.m. for two nights. There is nothing quieter than Alameda at night. In the end I shot video of the house about every 45 minutes and found nothing. Again, the key is to find out as soon as possible if the client is for real, and if they have the resources to commit to an investigation. I tell them that police put teams of four and five detectives for weeks at a time on big cases, which costs a ton of money. I do try to find cheaper solutions, but at a certain point, if you want answers, you have to commit.

In my younger days I didn't have the leverage or the money to turn down cases. But bad decisions make for good stories. One ill-fated job choice played out early in my career, when a client hired me to take photos of a rival ad company that he felt had stolen his packaging designs. This case was in 1996 or 1997, before digital cameras. I walked into the open lobby of the rival company, and while no one was at the reception desk I took some pictures with a manual Pentax camera. I might as well have been lighting firecrackers because the camera's loud clicks in the quiet office brought a worker back out front to catch me in the act with my camera. He grabbed me while I reached for his throat. I told him he better just call the cops before things escalated. Police showed up to arrest me for trespassing and confiscated my film. I beat the case because my client's attorney correctly argued that I had been taking pictures in a place accessible to the general public, and therefore my actions did not constitute trespassing. We got the film returned. The packaging at issue was in plain view. Part of me still wishes I had put that dweeb in a headlock when I had the chance.

But more often, I try to stick to more dignified assignments that won't get me in fights or land me in police handcuffs. I still like adventure. And what says adventure like digging through garbage looking for evidence?

Yes, dumpster diving. The mission works best applied to single-family homes or in places where you can know for sure that it's your subject's garbage you'll be sifting through. My M.O. is to go late, like 2 a.m., with a driver or an assistant and a replacement trash bag. I sit in the car while the assistant grabs the garbage. One freezing night in Napa, my assistant Cornelius—about six feet four inches, all legs and elbows—grabbed some trash bags and hoofed it back to the car. As I was keeping an eye on the rearview I heard bottles hitting the pavement as Cornelius sprinted—the paper trash bags had broken through the bottom. Cornelius scooped up what he could and we just hauled ass out of the area. Another time I brought along with me my friend Pete the Big

Animal, a former rugby colleague, on a case looking into a counterfeit purse operation in Daly City. Pete simply scooped up all the evidence in his giant arms and plopped it into my trunk. (If my wife is away, I will put the trash in my bathtub and sort through material wearing work gloves or rubber gloves. If she is home, I will sort it out in the back yard.)

Another quick Cornelius story. I had papers to serve on an elusive subject and had finally ascertained where he was staying up in the Oakland hills. Cornelius was a Berkeley student at the time, a gamer and prone to late-night partying; process serving is best done early in the morning so as to catch the targets by surprise. We chased after this guy as he was evading and a severely hungover Cornelius managed to drive alongside him, give him his notice, and fling the papers into the bed of his pickup truck.

All this work has led me to a steady practice. I've built a good reputation by taking on tough assignments. One such niche is "difficult service of process"—I can charge full freight for finding and serving a person routine servers have already failed to zap. Serving papers on the Archbishop of San Francisco at mass the day before he took a promotion to the Vatican ranks as my favorite. He had been the archbishop in Portland and was a witness in a suit attorneys had brought against the Church in connection with pedophile priests. I had left numerous messages with his office informing him that he had to be served and that I wanted to handle this discretely. I had grown up an altar boy in the church, my parents are devout Catholics, and I wanted to approach the matter with some decorum. But with no response by phone I started looking for him near his offices. With time running out, the only way to serve him would be just before he said his last mass in San Francisco. I walked up to him and announced that he could be served now or during mass. I don't think he swore at me, but he seemed close to dropping an F-bomb. He and his office subsequently tried to spin it to the media that it was an outrage to be served in the church, failing to mention that he had turned down plenty of earlier opportunities to accept the papers.

In all, a career as a private investigator entails a combination of business sense, street smarts, client management, savviness, and straight-up attitude; while the job varies from month-to-month (and day-to-day), the constant in the equation is *me*. If I don't use good judgment in everything I do, not only does my business suffer, but also my self-regard. I'd rather live with a smaller paycheck than with compromised integrity.

CHAPTER 6

HOW I LEARNED TO SCREEN CLIENTS: THE CASE OF GARY VINCENT MURPHY

ON A RAINY FEBRUARY DAY, Betty, a husky-voiced woman in her late 50s pounded a margarita in my neighborhood Mexican restaurant. It felt like a movie scene. I was there meeting her in person so that she could sign a contract—and put down a $1,000 retainer. She was hiring me to get dirt on Gary Vincent Murphy, who had fathered her granddaughter, Amy, a pretty blond girl. The girl's mother (i.e., the client's daughter) had died of an accidental overdose, and a battle was raging for custody of the little girl. Even before the case ended when Gary Murphy was found murdered, John Nazarian and I almost went to jail over our handling of the case.

I planned to obtain information on Murphy, a convicted drug dealer and parolee, through surveillance. Betty gave me photos of Murphy so I would know my subject. She described him as a depraved father caught up in sex and drugs, not fit to be a parent. My heart was immediately invested in this case. How could I let this innocent little girl be raised by such a monster?

But almost from the beginning of the case I got the sense I was hearing mixed messages. In one of the photos, Murphy looked like a pirate: fabulous, glossy black hair in a ponytail, a bushy black beard, a sparkling, toothy grin, and a sleeve of tattoos down one arm. In the photo, he stood in front of an old brown station wagon cradling his daughter, who clasped him around the neck and gazed right into his eyes with a huge smile. In the other photo, the little girl sat at a table with her parents to celebrate what was maybe a fifth or sixth birthday. She wore pink and had just received a pink lunchbox as a present. Murphy, the mother, and the little girl all had natural smiles; the picture of young family bliss.

I began the search for dirt on Murphy and his associates at the San Francisco and Alameda County criminal and civil courts. The San Francisco Hall of Justice, known simply as The Hall, hasn't changed much over the years. It's a seven-story gray slab at 850 Bryant Street that houses the San Francisco police administration and detective bureaus, criminal and traffic courts, and criminal records, with the county jail occupying the top two floors. Criminal records at that time were on the first and fourth floors, muni court or lesser crimes on the first floor, and serious stuff or superior court cases up on the fourth floor. (Since then all records have been consolidated on the first floor.) I found a couple Murphy case files up on the fourth floor. His most recent stint in prison had been come after the cops caught him red-handed with a few pounds of meth in a room equipped with police scanners, and possibly some weapons. He had taken a plea deal that sent him to state prison for a few years and landed him on parole for about three years. This was his second drug-related felony, so all things considered he got off with a light prison term.

The client told me that Murphy still ran with a rough crowd of bikers. After staking out the place where he and Betty met to exchange the little girl for custody visits, I followed him on surveillance. I learned that he would stay with a Harley-riding blond woman in a luxurious loft near the San Francisco end of the Bay Bridge (I watched him from a spot near the scene from Hitchcock's *Vertigo* with the view of the Bay Bridge). However, I never saw him doing anything illegal.

Concurrently with the surveillance I continued my research at the Alameda County courts. While I didn't find any additional incriminating information on my subject, I did unearth some bad information about my client. In the bowels of Oakland's Rene C. Davidson courthouse, a stately building overlooking Lake Merritt, I found two restraining orders against Betty. In the first, her granddaughter's preschool filed a restraining order against her for making threats against staff members, perhaps relating to a payment issue. In the second restraining order, which had been taken out against her by Murphy a few years prior, he accused her of showing up at his place and threatening him. The court order apparently was never granted as neither party had showed up for subsequent hearings. This was the first big case where I had cause to worry about my client's motives, but I was not about to bring up the matter of these restraining orders with her—first, she was paying me, and secondly, while the court files hinted at her temper, she had never actually faced criminal charges.

Meanwhile, Betty was getting restless over my lack of progress in the surveillance of Murphy. As a practical matter, watching someone for 10 or 20 hours isn't always a sufficient amount of time for identifying associates or determining criminal behavior. I always remind clients that I can't tell them what happens behind closed doors. In hopes of advancing the case, I brought in Nazarian. I set up another meeting with Betty, telling her that I would be enlisting my more senior associate.

Nazarian came over to my apartment before we went together to Betty's house. The client told us we would get a big bonus on top of another retainer if Murphy was arrested and we helped her win in the child custody fight. Betty claimed to know prison bad-asses and hinted that she could get them to plant drugs on Murphy. Nazarian assured her that he would mobilize his associates in the police to stop and search Murphy, thereby catching him in violation of his parole. Nazarian's words had their effect (maybe his sinister goatee helped); Betty immediately went to the freezer and pulled out a Ritz cracker box stuffed with about $15,000 in cash. The bulk of the retainer went to Nazarian. A few weeks later, Betty lashed out at us for not doing our jobs, because Murphy was not yet behind bars. She was not satisfied with my surveillance efforts, and Nazarian had exaggerated to her about what he might be able to do with his police contacts. With Betty increasingly volcanic, we informed her we would be dropping her as a client. We kept copies of her nasty notes to us and our written responses to her, and felt relief at escaping from a bad situation.

Wrong! Three months after kicking Betty to the curb (or was it she who had kicked us?) as I sat in my apartment reading the *San Francisco Examiner*, I stumbled upon a news brief that Gary Vincent Murphy had been murdered in a San Francisco halfway house. A masked assailant had chased him on foot and gunned him down with a pistol. I felt sick to my stomach, and my head started to ache. I managed to find a little solace—and an alibi—in the fact that the place where Murphy was killed was not a location I had previously tracked him, and therefore it was not through me that my client had potentially discovered his whereabouts.

Nazarian and I immediately went to the San Francisco police homicide unit to give statements. The detective, who looked like Detective

Mark Fuhrman from the O.J. Simpson case, interviewed me for almost three hours; the police initially suspected that John and I might have had something to do with the death. Independently, our accounts checked out that we had nothing to do with the murder. I can't blame police for their suspicions; after all, I did have the victim under surveillance at various times, and we had worked for a client with a motive. Who knows what would have happened if Nazarian and I had not met together with the client? If I had just taken the case myself, I could have been made the patsy, and it would have been my word against hers.

The murder remained unsolved, and I later heard that Betty had moved back to her native Canada shortly afterward. I looked up the victim's father, a prominent Boston attorney and World War II hero who has since died, and called him up to tell him my side of the story. Then, just last year, I got a phone call from Amy, who is now in her early 20s, with her mother's beauty and her father's tattoos. At no point during or after the investigation had I ever heard from her up until then. I'm still not sure why she tracked me down and reached out, but she wanted to talk. She confided that her childhood had been tough. Growing up, her father's side of the family seldom spoke of his death, while Betty's side would tell her he had died in an accident. She hadn't even known he had been murdered until she started doing her own Internet research and found the *Bay Guardian* article from many years ago about her father's case, written by the investigative reporter A.C. Thompson. I offered what comfort I could, telling her that her father must have loved her very much because of how they appeared together in those old photos. I still had the photos in my file and gave them to her. She also dropped the news that Betty had moved back to the Bay Area.

To this day, the murder remains a mystery. My own connection and involvement in the case gnaws at me and always will. I look at it as a stain on my professional record. It also soured me a bit on working for private clients. People don't hire private investigators because their lives are going well; they hire us because they have enemies or other serious problems. As a new or young private investigator you do take lumps in figuring out who makes for a worthwhile client. Sometimes, the pursuit of a paycheck leads you into strange places and exposes you to people you would never otherwise meet. I would tell any private investigator that you better screen all your potential clients. Don't let yourself be blinded by a quick buck. This case made me realize the seriousness of my work, and I don't want a case like it again.

CHAPTER 7

DEALING WITH
CROOKS, CONS, AND SCUM

A L AND HIS NEPHEW met me many times at the El Pollo Loco on
International Boulevard, as it's now called. To old-timers it's East
14th Street, but 20 years ago Oakland tried to put lipstick on a pig by
giving the boulevard a new name. The streetwalkers still strut day and
night just north of El Pollo Loco. After ordering at the counter we hit the
buffet-style spread of salsas and vegetables.

"So, Mike, you got any new information? I mean, you got anything
really good you can tell me?" Al asked when his nephew left the table
for more chips and dip. And I would lay out my progress, complete with
a report or maybe a VHS tape of the footage shot with my 8-millimeter
camera, this being the tech of the day back in 1998. Al was so pleased
with my work that in addition to a handful of Benjamins, he presented
me with a brand-new leather briefcase that I used for at least a decade. Al
was short, fat and almost 70 years old, with gray hair and dancing brown
eyes. He later died of a heart attack. To this day I think fondly of him and
am forever in debt to him for introducing me to El Pollo Loco.

Al's family and extended family had lived in Oakland-San Francisco
for generations. They were members of the Rom, also known as Roma
or Romany people (known pejoratively as "gypsies."), who originated in
India 1500 years ago and spread throughout Europe and subsequently
the world. Of course, it would be a cheap stereotype to characterize
all Roma as crooked fortunetellers and grifters. But, as with any ethnic
group, a tiny segment of the population in California engages in a range
of frauds, from welfare and Social Security scams, to selling junk used
cars, to personal injury shakedown lawsuits, to sweetheart scams against
the elderly. For all I know, Al and some of his family were just as crooked

as the kin he had me investigating. But he was my client, I liked him, and he had my loyalty. (In case you haven't noticed, I eventually come to like almost all my clients.)

Al wanted dirt on his in-laws, George and Sylvia Yonko of Berkeley. Al had a daughter who had married into the Yonko family, and he blamed them for her prison time. When families wage war on their own kind, it's as if they are competitive crooks: if one scores big, the others want to take him down. Al and his family lived at the bottom of High Street in Oakland while the Yonkos had a place off Ashby Avenue near the I-80 freeway in Berkeley and another place near the Ashby BART train station.

The case stands out as one of the first in which I would work side-by-side with law enforcement. At the same time I was obliged to wear a few hats and run a few ruses to protect my client. It's also a stark reminder that there are people out there willing to target the elderly with financial fraud, a truly despicable crime that shames and destroys the trust and dignity of our society's elders.

I began the investigation in Berkeley with surveillance on the cars on and around the Yonko house on Ashby Avenue. They were driving white, new GMC Yukons with "paper plates," that is, dealership plates. Recording the vehicle identification numbers involved climbing on top of the vehicles to photograph each number, which is not optimal for stealth. A VIN is usually written on a little piece of metal below the windshield or on the inset of a door. From the VINs I determined that the cars belonged to a few different dealerships in Las Vegas and were almost certainly stolen.

I needed some more data in addition to the VINs. For this I turned to my best investigative technique of the day: phone records. Obtaining phone records was not patently illegal at the time, and it often proved to be one of the most reliable sources of information. Because I acquired the numbers through an information broker, there was no clear impropriety on my end.

With phone records, I look for two things: phone numbers repeatedly called and duration of calls. Repeated outgoing calls and longer calls signify an ongoing relationship. The next step is to learn the identities behind the phone numbers and their addresses. With the Yonkos, I found at least a dozen numbers of potential interest.

As with any investigation, I conducted a background check on my subject down at the local courthouse. I learned that an elderly man, John Franklin, had sued George Yonko claiming that the latter owed him $30,000 from an investment in a drapery deal business in Las Vegas on which Yonko and his family had reneged. I did a bit more research and recognized that Mr. Franklin number was one of those in the Yonko phone records.

A few of the other Yonko phone records also had Las Vegas lines. As much as I would have relished flying to Vegas to track these people down, I needed a Nevada-licensed private investigator—investigating in a state where you are not licensed can get you in legal trouble and other sticky situations. Therefore, I contracted with Heidi Johnson of Ally Investigations. Heidi did great work and found two or three victims and interviewed them. It seemed that George and Sylvia had deployed their daughters in the oldest of cons: the sweetheart scam. The girls would target men 50 and older in the grocery store and move in, feigning romantic interest. They would cultivate a relationship and over time start hitting up the old-timers for money, purportedly for someone in the family needing an operation for cancer. In the Yonko ruse, the story was that the young women had been offered a great business opportunity for the contract to supply draperies at a major hotel but needed the capital to buy the supplies, with the hint of romance played up for the lonely old men. Heidi found that the Las Vegas victims had co-signed on the new Yukons that I had been investigating in Berkeley. She also got a statement that the Yonkos had literally held one of the victims down in the back of the Yukon and used needle-nose pliers to remove a gold wedding band they couldn't get off his finger. That kind of detail of cruelty against a victim personalizes a case and hardens my resolve to destroy the bad guy, or bad girl.

All these events and leads surfaced at about the same time. In Oakland-Berkeley I began knocking on doors of other potential Yonko victims. At the time I was dating a good-looking woman, and I brought her along with me to check out the possible victims—most people will talk to a woman before they talk to a salty private dick, but he showed little interest in talking to me or to her. However, he did acknowledge he was a victim who had lost everything. I have seen a lot and have learned to be skeptical about even more, but he had such a profound sadness in his eyes, face and whole being. Not only did he have his savings stolen; they had taken his dignity as well.

I had enough to call the district attorney, and I also had an idea to go after and get the Yonkos, if not sending them straight to hell maybe making them miserable. I'm even keeled when I go after people. It's an intellectual exercise. But this case was different. Maybe it's because I don't have kids and will be old very soon or love my elderly parents, but crimes against the elderly make me psycho.

John Franklin, the guy who had sued George Yonko for about $30,000, would act as my ploy. I noted in the court file that Franklin had never collected from the Yonkos. I called Bart Rothman, an attorney, and brought him on board. Rothman would represent Franklin in a collections effort against the Yonkos. The incentive for Rothman was that if he could collect from the Yonkos, he would get a percentage of the fee due to Franklin. With enough pressure from Rothman and me, for example, veiled threats of going to the cops, Yonko might be willing to settle with Franklin and Rothman. My ultimate motive, however, was to get closer to the Yonkos in order to gather evidence against them on behalf of not only my client Al but on behalf of all their other victims.

I called the consumer protection branch of the Alameda County DA's office. They put me through to one of the best investigators I have ever met, Kathy Boyovich. It turned out that Boyovich and I had been following a parallel investigative path and knew about the same victims. What I didn't know was the scale and volume: as I learned from Boyovich, the Yonko family had taken Franklin and ten other victims, ages 73 to 89, for a total of $1.3 million over five years with a stream of cons of fake drapery and sham olive oil businesses. I shared all of my video and the statements from Las Vegas victims with the DA's office.

Meanwhile, Rothman drafted new legal papers for me to serve on George Yonko. I knew there would be trouble so I had my girlfriend come with me to keep the engine running as I attempted the serve. Some serves are simple but others feel more like a fight. It's important to have an exit plan and exit route. My heartbeat increased as I approached the house on foot, even more so when I rapped on their heavy metal-screen door. I had the papers in hand but shifted my weight to my heels, ready to turn and run. George Yonko opened the door after my first knock and along with his beefy son tried to grab me and drag me inside. I fought them off with a series of hand motions and thrusts like a wide receiver swatting a defensive back attempting to jam him at the line of scrimmage. In the tumult I managed to inform George that he was being served and dropped the papers at his feet. I ran to my girlfriend's waiting car and we sped away.

A few months passed. The DA on the case called me with a plan to have me wear a wire in order to record George Yonko making a statement about defrauding Franklin and other victims. On a gray spring day I went to the DA's satellite office on Oakport near the Oakland Coliseum. Boyovich fitted me with the recording device in my waistband, running the wire up to the mic taped to my chest. Yonko had agreed to meet me at the old Chevy's restaurant on the water near Jack London Square, under the pretense that I was seeking to work out a payment plan for Franklin. Boyovich reassured me that she and other DA investigators would be in a car in a nearby parking lot listening to our talk. I was supposed to say something like "Super Bowl" as my safe word if I needed immediate help. I was nervous, but such was my disgust for the Yonkos that I was more than willing to play my part to trap George. I found him inside and got right down to business. He was a small balding man with salt-and-pepper hair and beady eyes. Try as I might, I could not get Yonko to incriminate himself. I confronted him with my knowledge about his schemes, but he just danced out of the corner like a skilled boxer.

Yonko won that small battle, but in due course law enforcement landed on him and his family in an unprecedented prosecution. Facing a mountain of evidence, George and his wife each pleaded to 10 years in prison in 2001. I never had to testify in open court. The scope of the criminal case against them was unheard because of the length of the sentence and because of the restrictions the court put on the children of the defendants.

A condition of the plea was that the Yonkos would keep their children out of prison if the children agreed to using only one identity each, learned to read and write, stayed in school, and swore off the con-artist lifestyle of their parents.

And yet, George and his wife might be back to working their scams. Recently, while I was working on another fraud case, a Santa Clara County DA informed me that George and Sylvia have relocated to San

Jose and have resumed plying their old cons. Their kids pop up in the news every now and then on the local news investigative segments.

Since the Yonkos, I have handled over a half-dozen similar con-artist cases. In one such case a family hired me to intervene with their daughter who had been conned out of more than $60,000 by an East Bay psychic. It was a classic psychic ploy: in return for your money, they will burn a candle on a mountaintop or in a graveyard and when the candle is gone so is the cancer, bad luck, curse, acne, or flatulence. I asked investigator Kathy Boyovich for her help. Only then did I realize the degree of her dedication: despite having retired two days prior from more than 30 years with the DA's office, while needing meniscus surgery on her knee from a work-related injury, she had jumped at the chance to help yet another victim. We staked out the victim's apartment waiting for her to come home so we could have a word with her. A moving crew had propped open the front door to the building. In a flash I saw our subject and ran to the door, Boyovich limping gingerly after me. The victim denied knowing the psychics, but it was clear that Boyovich had her attention, and that the young woman was rattled. We left after talking to her for about a half hour.

The victim's parents were the ones who had hired us. We did our best on a limited retainer to stage an intervention to warn the young woman against the psychics. Whether she eventually came to her senses, whether she realized her parents had hired us, or whether she kept throwing away good money on a bunch of crooks, I do not know. After the retainer was depleted, the parents didn't want to pay us more, which is not uncommon—some cases just fizzle out because of lack of funds. I can only hope Boyovich and I performed a successful intervention. Maybe I should have called the client for a follow-up, but as is often the case I was already on to the next customer.

In the big picture for a big city, crooked psychics chiseling people for a few thousand here and there doesn't merit a good deal of law enforcement attention. Still, as with most crimes, it's not an issue until you or a loved one is a victim.

CHAPTER 8

FINDING THE INVISIBLE MAN—
THE MISSING MILLIONAIRE

I N THE PSYCHIC AND CON-ARTIST CASES, I am investigating an adversary who has stolen thousands, even millions of dollars. But in other cases, I am tracking down people who stand to inherit millions.

This story begins with me walking up to a house on a case. An elfin, bearded man in blue pajamas clutching a black and white cat came out and walked up to the cyclone fence. "Want to buy my bicycle?" he asked.

"No, not really. Can I talk to your landlord? And who are you?"

"I'm Bucky. Do you have any money so I can buy cat food?" It was one of those breezy, sunny summer days in the East Bay, a comfortable 65 degrees. I told him that I only had $5 on me, reached into my pocket and handed it to him.

Such was my introduction to the man known as Bucky. The case had come to me from an East Coast private investigator working for a trust attorney. Bucky, then in his 60s, had not been seen by any of his family members in more than 25 years. In fact, the only proof he was alive were a few letters and emails—that is, if they were truly from him. Bucky's mother had a sizeable estate and was sending him monthly checks for $3,000 or $4,000 to an address in Oakland or to a PO Box in Berkeley. The checks were being cashed at the same bank. Bucky's brother killed himself and left him more than $100,000. The attorney sent email and letters to Bucky that he would have to come forward with identification if he wanted to collect on the brother's estate. Bucky did not come forward but sent a couple emails, originating out of Texas, to the attorney, stating he did not want to come forward. So, he presumably was alive. Then, Bucky's mother died and left him more than $7 million. The attorney sent more letters and emails and hired the East Coast private eye who in turn hired me.

We had a genuine mystery. Was Bucky alive? Was he the one cashing the checks? Why would he not want to come forward and claim all the money?

The East Coast P.I. had already got underway with the hard work. The digital divide looms large: people over a certain age don't live on the Internet. There were a couple of possible hits from Bucky on web sites and blogs, but those were from over a decade ago. Bucky had grown up attending the finest prep schools and a private college, but subsequently he had cut all ties from the stuffy East. He flew free and, based on the evidence on the blogs, embraced a nomadic lifestyle of traveling around the country in a van. We did all the basics to try to locate Bucky, including:

- Running his Social Security number. Nothing showed that he used it in the last 20 years. A couple of names came back under his SSN, and I interviewed them; they knew nothing. Credit bureaus make mistakes.
- Checking whether he had a driver's license. He had one in California more than 20 years ago but surrendered it in New Mexico. He also had vehicles registered to him in Alaska more than 20 years ago. We learned from the licenses that he would be about six-foot-two.
- Checking criminal, civil, and traffic courts in all the states where he had lived. Nothing. Also checking the federal Pacer index for criminal, civil, and bankruptcy records. Zip.
- Searching for surviving relatives with whom to check. There were none.
- Looking for cell phones, utilities, or cable registered under his name. Again, nothing.
- Contacting the alumni office from his college. No updates.
- Searching all the main social media and online resources. No hits other than the old blog posts.
- Searching online death indexes. Nothing there.
- I even checked with a law enforcement source. Nothing in the computers ever, nationwide for Bucky, not even a traffic stop or jaywalking citation.

A number of bizarre scenarios presented themselves. Maybe Bucky had got a hold of someone else's SSN and date of birth and had created a whole new identify for himself? Or perhaps someone else had gained Bucky's confidence and gleaned enough information to write those letters and the emails to the attorney? What if poor Bucky had died in a ditch in the high desert and his bleached white bones were all that was left of him?

The search turned to Oakland and the East Bay, my stomping grounds. I contracted for some surveillance down at the place where the checks had been sent to him, a spooky area next to a freeway, bordering on a recycling plant. We ran license plates parked near the house: nothing relevant. No signs of present occupation. Weeds and plants obscured a view of the house, a chain and lock prevented access. I interviewed past residents of that address; they had never heard of Bucky. Focus shifted to the landlord, and although nothing sinister came up on him in a public records check, we held off approaching him out of concern that perhaps the landlord was the one cashing the checks. I dropped by the house a couple times in person to poke around for clues: nothing. I even had one of my former high school rugby players, a Mexican kid, do a pretext looking for yard work, but he couldn't get anyone to answer.

We reached the end of our rope, and it came time to try to interview the landlord. In this business you don't call to schedule appointments for an interview, because that leads to blow-offs. The best technique is a "hot show"—surprise them at the door and hope to get them talking.

That summer day, rather than approaching the house from the street again, I got the idea of walking through the recycling plant parking lot, where a corner of the back yard was accessible. To my delight, I found a bicycle with a "for sale" sign resting against the fence. This part of the yard and house was invisible to surveillance from the street. Had I not approached from the hidden angle, I would not have found Bucky—and Bucky might not have become a millionaire.

I told him the reason for my visit. He explained that all along he had been receiving and cashing the checks, until the attorney stopped sending them during our attempts to verify his whereabouts and identity. Bucky had also been receiving all the correspondence from the attorney, but explained that he had not come forward because he did not have a valid driver's license, which was required by a notary in order to sign the papers to start collecting the inheritances. The East Coast P.I. had located college yearbook photos and sent them to me; it was definitely Bucky. He is a sound, pleasant guy who does a lot of bike riding.

We had found our man, and all that remained were some minor procedural hoops to jump through before he could collect his fortune. The Bucky matter took a bit more time to resolve, however, due to his reluctance to obtain proper identification. The lawyers and court back East want him to get an official California identification card. Bucky just says he will "go back east" when he gets around to it and bristles at the prospects of applying for an official ID. After annoying Bucky on a few further occasions by dropping by unannounced, he finally agreed to answer a series of questions from the attorney to prove his identity. He will live out his remaining years wealthy, perhaps content to stay in his back yard home near the freeway and the recycling plant.

* * *

Bucky's case was easy in terms of ethics; to find him, all I had to do was make use of publicly available information, put in some legwork, and draw from my past experience. But not every case is so easy in determining right from wrong. I have a sliding scale of ethics, like many people in my profession (and probably yours). Any private eye worth his salt has tricks up his or her sleeve, resources cultivated and hoarded for years. What amuses me is the holier-than-thou private eye who purports to speak for the industry, claiming we are all Boy Scouts pledged to do no wrong. If they aren't hypocrites, these self-appointed spokespeople are not very effective investigators. The public has never quite trusted private investigators, but the modern private dick is much more clever, educated, and resourceful than his predecessors. A good private investigator is like a good defensive back or linebacker who knows exactly what the rules and penalties are and will go right up to that line to test the referee and his opposition. He is careful to get back on the right side of the ball or remove his hands just in time to avoid being caught offside or committing a penalty.

When a case is going to play out in court, I avoid using any tactics that might be perceived as shady or underhanded or unethical. If I am expected to testify honestly about my methods, I won't partake in questionable activities. When you are dealing with a criminal defense or a civil matter, there is no room for lying or shading the truth. You will be found out and embarrassed. I have nothing but contempt for any cop or expert or investigator who lies under oath. You either have professional integrity, or you don't. Needless to say, I have experienced my share of friction with attorneys who didn't like my honest testimony or my refusal to shade or quibble.

For this reason, I find that I have more freedom to unleash resources in cases in which I am hired to locate a missing loved one or find a missing heir who might have money coming their way.

My trick? Information brokers. They have access to information on employment histories, credit accounts, utilities, bank accounts, phone records, and so on. About the only things they can't get are medical records and tax returns; obtaining those would be a felony. Still, I only use information brokers for good causes. Many private investigators and lawyers have been hung out to dry because they used information brokers in an attempt to win at all costs. For example, there was the infamous Hewlett Packard scandal, in which HP hired a law firm who used Action Research of Florida in order to identify the source of a leak to the press. The problem was that Action Research used pretexts to illicitly obtain phone records of reporters and others involved in the case. Confession: before all this hit the fan, Action was commonly used by private investigators, myself included, to get phone records. But the times and laws were changing. I stopped using Action because I could see that it was only a matter of time before the legality of what they were doing would come into question. Inevitably, the HP case made all the national papers and resulted in new laws. The father and son from Florida pleaded to aggravated identity theft and got three years' probation, and the fallout left a wide wake. While I could still get someone's phone records without a court order (illegally) through information brokers—everything is for sale—I choose not to because a few thousand bucks is not worth a felony.

In most cases, information brokers are not licensed as private investigators. They tend to be located in states such as Colorado, Texas, Missouri, and Florida with minimal oversight of private investigators and affiliated professions. My assumption is that they get their information through "inside sources" at utility companies, credit agencies, banks, and the like, as well as from "social engineering"—a euphemism for tricking employees into breaking security procedures and providing sensitive information.

I am currently on about my seventh information broker, though I use a total of three of them concurrently depending on what I need. Of those I used formerly, one failed me three times. After charging me for no results for the third time, they sent me a pre-printed apology card and a couple chocolate chip cookies. Did they really have cards and cookies ready to send upon failing to deliver?

Another information broker, this one located in Missouri, whom I worked with for a short time was producing great results. On one case where I was having difficulty serving papers to an elusive subject, the broker was able to tell me the precise shop where the subject regularly bought her wine. We served her, wine in hand. I had to break off relations with the broker when I ran my own background on him and uncovered his history of meth arrests, larceny, and child abuse.

I went to Florida last year to meet with my latest information broker, a former collections executive for a major Las Vegas casino. A fellow P.I. had referred me to him. We met at a Cheesecake Factory near the Tampa Airport. Remember, all shady—as well as good—meetings occur near airports; better yet, at bars near airports. This broker is a short, balding guy in his late 60s, likes cigarettes and tennis, and wears gold jewelry. He has been in the information business for more than 15 years. I can give him a hotel room number, and he can give me the name of the person who paid for the room. He can also tell me what prescription medicine someone takes. He confided to me that the federal justice department and other federal agencies use his services.

My big gripe with information brokers, though, is that they are the flakiest mothers under the sun. They pull the rabbit out of the hat by telling you where a certain someone buys their liquor but then on the next case they won't return your call for two weeks rather than admit they have failed. They are brokers because they have their sources. But sources dry up; it's a constant exercise to find a good broker.

I do not mess with hacking email or with obtaining banking, financial, or medical records without a judgment, or with any avenues of research prohibited by federal and other laws. I suppose there are information brokers and private investigators who do such things, but it's just not worth it to me. On the other hand, if a client does have a court judgment against someone, then I might contract out to a private eye who specializes in asset searches. Phone records are another area I steer clear of. In the old days many an unscrupulous P.I. or broker would simply pretext the phone company that their bill got rained on in the mailbox and request a new one. All of these avenues—banking records, phone records, emails—are powerful investigative tools, but due to their sensitivity most courts require subpoenas for such information.

* * *

The caller from San Mateo told me she wanted to find her missing brother because their father was on his deathbed. She had hired a local private investigator before, but he had failed, and time was running out. I took the case not exactly knowing whether I could produce. She explained that the siblings of her Japanese-American family used to be close but how hurt they were by his absence; they had not heard from him in seven years and dad was about to die, and mom likely wouldn't be long in following him. For me to take a case I have to like the potential client. I come from a large family and could sympathize. She sounded serious and normal. She passed all my sniff tests.

I did all the regular steps: checking public records, commercial databases, free people-search web sites, in-person visits to the courts. Nothing. I called a broker I had used since my Nazarian days. I will refer to the broker as Martin.

Within a day or two Martin reported that the subject was possibly working at a restaurant in San Diego. With the client's permission I flew down to San Diego. I love it when clients pay me to travel. That's when I feel like I'm living the real private eye lifestyle, however bizarre the case may be. This time I'd be there for just a couple days working on obtaining video that would prove he was our missing subject.

I am good at spotting in person people whose faces I have seen only in a photo. For example, ears are unique, like fingerprints. An old San Francisco P.I., Paul Kangas, once told me to pay attention to ears when trying to identify someone. Following his method, I've found that he was right. I once found a runaway teenager in Berkeley by watching a crowd of hundreds of kids, specifically their ears, as they emerged from a high school until I saw the right pair. Harder to explain are "gut feelings"; I put my trust in them and often enough they turn out to be right. After a week of searching unsuccessfully for a woman, I coincidentally saw her as I was exiting my gym. I did not have the photo handy, but I just knew it was her. I followed her on foot to her car, then followed her to where she lived. It's almost as if, when I need to win, I find a way.

Back to the missing brother in San Diego. I found him working in a sushi joint in a downscale part of town, north of the airport. I staked out the parking lot. I knew I had him. I followed him back to his apartment, noted the laundry hanging on the back porch, then beat it back to the hotel. Despite my trust in my gut, I had to be patient and keep watching him to be 100-percent I had the right man.

When I'm on surveillance as I was in San Diego, I see the minute, pedestrian rhythms of life. There is something comforting about watching life play out from my car's front seat. The bond between private investigator and his vehicle cannot be overestimated. As one veteran P.I. once said at a conference, "Your car is your little duck blind." He also spoke about the bond between the P.I. and his coffee machine: "I'm a Swede so I go through coffee machines like other people change shirts."

After doing some surveillance day and night in San Diego I would go back to my hotel and have a drink or two, watch ESPN or a movie, and call my wife. Repeated trips to the restaurant parking lot and his apartment established his daily routine: he lived a quiet life, alone and hard-working. After a few days I could confirm that I had the right man. Mission accomplished!

Normally, the industry's "best practices" would be to notify the subject and ask whether they wanted to be contacted by their relative or whoever was the client. But this case was different. I took the client at her word that her family needed this information as soon as possible. I gave her the skinny on her brother. A few weeks later she told me that she and her sister had made the trip to San Diego and had a great reunion with their brother. They brought him back in touch with their elderly parents, just in time. (I generally don't do what is known in the trade as "nostalgia locates" for people trying to find lost loves or old friends. Relationships end for a reason: if the estranged ones wanted to get in touch with you, they would do so on their own initiative!)

Another memorable missing-persons matter involved a client who had not been in touch with her brother in about a decade. Same scenario: the parents were about to die. I contacted an information broker who passed me a tip that the subject might be paying utilities at a place in Palmdale in rural northern Los Angeles County. The local sheriff had looked for him on a welfare check but couldn't locate him. To find him I would have to drive down myself to the scrub and desert.

Oakland has a temperate climate, but on the July day I set off on my drive it was 90. As I went east through Pleasanton and Modesto and then headed south it was about 100. I drove my Infiniti I-30 six-cylinder sedan at about 75 miles per hour. In Fresno it hit 105. By the time I reached Bakersfield it was 110. I drove over the Grapevine, the connector of Interstate 5 to Southern California, at 117 degrees. I prayed my car engine would not quit. I turned off the air conditioning on the steepest part of the climb. I could feel the swamp-butt effect on the leather seats. I hung a left and drove another hour or so to a hotel.

It seems as if whatever address I'm looking for will never be clearly marked or easy to find. All next day I drove around in the heat looking for the house. Finally that evening, after the heat broke and went under 100, I found it, basically a shack, on a farm property. He was there, living with a partner. He was in bad physical condition, he possibly had AIDS. I put him back in touch with his sister. Another case where I was able to use a broker to get good information for a good cause.

Potential clients always want to know how much an investigation will cost and how long it will take. I tell them that every case is different and suggest a retainer to try to see how far I will get within an initial budget. There are just too many variables to give them a solid estimate. It's not like I am replacing a clutch or a water pump or a leaky faucet.

In the Internet age, where all kinds of personal information is just a Google search away, why should anybody hire a private investigator in the first place? John and Jane Square who have jobs and a mortgage are easy to locate using the free or cheap searches, such as Spokeo, Radaris, Zaba, even easier if you're looking for someone with an uncommon name. But the more unstable a person is, the harder they are to find. As I'm writing this, I just tested Spokeo on myself; it reported my "current" address as a place on Martin Luther King Jr. Way in Oakland where I lived 20 years ago. As P.I.s, however, we have access to more robust databases that are drawn from a wider range of relevant sources, such as cable and other utilities, and are updated more frequently. If the cheap stuff fails a local private eye and put him or her on a strict budget.

As with society as a whole, we private investigators are more dependent than ever on databases, computers, and technology. While the volume of digital information has swelled exponentially, the Internet is not always the final answer. Any piece of information will always have to be confirmed by the senses, as in the example of spotting a man and his cat in an unlisted back yard near an Oakland freeway. Shoe leather and "eyes on" intelligence are still perhaps the most important forms of gathering information. Think of it this way: A GPS device tells you where a particular vehicle or cell phone might be, but it provides no context. Who is the person in the vehicle or with the phone, and what are they doing? You will not have any idea unless you observe the situation with your own eyes. As any good reporter will tell you, scoops don't come from hanging out in the newsroom—you have to go out and look for them! Decades after switching careers, I still do an awful lot of that on the job.

CHAPTER 9

MEN IN LOVE (AND LUST)
ARE FUNNY

IT WAS 4 A.M., and I was drifting in and out of sleep in a restaurant parking lot in Anaheim near Disneyland. I had to take a leak and wanted to shave my tongue. I stumbled from the rental car into the chill, pissed next to a dumpster, steam rose. I had hit my sleep wall, while my partner Elrod was stalking across vast territory on foot, searching for our client's missing needle of a car somewhere in that 160-acre haystack of a parking lot at Mouse Mecca. Elrod is a former Army Ranger and looking for a car in a parking lot was easier than scouting for the enemy in Iraq and Afghanistan where he served in combat. At about 5 a.m. he called me to say he hadn't found the car and was ready to be picked up. We drove the lonely highways back to a crappy hotel in Fullerton and knocked out for about four hours. At 45, I thought, am I too old for this? For the first time in my career I was thinking about aging, perhaps because of the contrast with Elrod, then a 29-year-old warrior badass. (Elrod and I used to play rugby together 13 years ago when he was a skinny redheaded teen-ager flashing anger and bravado all over the pitch.) But I really don't want to do any other work, I thought. I have my freedom and love my job. How many people can say this? Sure, I would like better cash flow at times, but I wake up with a work boner almost every day. Even in Fullerton.

This was also my first case involving a global positioning system (GPS). The case started when the client contacted us to research a young woman he had starting seeing. The young lady happened to be a prostitute, but he wanted a boyfriend-girlfriend relationship. He had given her one of his cars, worth about $29,000, but had changed his mind and wanted it back. He didn't have the nerve to just ask her or to simply take it back, so he came up with the idea to recover it secretly and let her think it had been stolen. As private investigators we avoid passing judgment on matters like these, especially when people pay good money. People make bad decisions in their personal lives and need help. I think the initial retainer was about $2,000, billed hourly at $125.

GPS was the obvious solution, although I didn't have one in stock. Because he was the registered owner of the car and his name was on the title, it was technically not illegal in California to plant such a device on *his* car. One day the client sent word that she would be visiting him at his apartment: a perfect time to install the GPS. But because we did not have time to order a high-quality unit, we had to make do with a model commercially available at Fry's Electronics, which unlike the more expensive units could not be wired to the car's battery; without a constant charge, it would run out of power after four or five days. The bigger problem was the crappy GPS; the device could only get the location down to a half-mile radius. Considering what we now have on our cell phones, the GPS at the time was a dinosaur. That said, we placed it on the undercarriage with double-sided Velcro. For the first day or two the car stayed locally in the Bay Area, but was not accessible to try a recovery.

That Friday night I was anticipating a nice dinner out with my wonderful wife. I got on the computer one more time to check. This time the car was not sitting in the Bay Area, but was rapidly driving south on Interstate 5, the main north-south freeway in California. "Elrod, we have a problem. It looks like the car is either at Los Alamitos Army Airfield or at Disneyland." We checked with the client. He wanted the car back and authorized us to fly to Orange County to attempt a recovery. We hopped on an 8 p.m. flight on Southwest.

That Saturday morning, following our all-night parking lot hunt, we were aware that the GPS signal would crap out in another 24 to 36 hours due to the low battery. We checked the computer and the monitor showed that the car had moved about 30 miles away, somewhere near Rowland Heights. Elrod and I grid-searched each and every block for about four hours. We knew we were close to the car. A funny thing about GPS, at least on our budget model: concrete interferes with the signal. It was getting late and I had to get back to Oakland on other business the next day, so Elrod dropped me off at the airport and continued his quest.

On Sunday I got a call from Elrod. "I found it but it's in a garage at a house, and I can't get access to it." A dilemma: he can partially see the car in an open garage at the end of the driveway. One additional issue here was that the client did not have a spare key to the car; the dealership had provided us with a code to get it started, but that involved entering a certain long code by a pattern of pulls on the hand brake. Even with cover to gain entry to the car, Elrod wouldn't have the time to play around with the brake code. I have known a handful of soldiers, Army, Marines and Navy. They are resourceful and deeply committed to getting results, and Elrod is no exception. But this was one of those things where a positive outcome would have to wait. I told him to come back home, and we would get it another time.

Having reported our close encounter to the client, he still wanted to stick with his plan to recover the car from his lady friend under the pretense of a theft. This time I invested in a higher-quality GPS unit, and the client arranged for us to install device while they went out for the day and she left the car parked in his garage. We assembled a kit consisting of duct tape, wire splicers, plastic tubing, and Velcro. Elrod's dad is a retired auto mechanic, so he knew a thing or two. I served as lookout while the master did his thing in about 40 minutes. Elrod spliced the GPS onto the car battery, disguising the wires in ordinary automotive tubing; this would give the unit a constant power supply, so the job wouldn't be time sensitive and we could wait for the optimal conditions for a recovery.

Elrod and I are on the same page when it comes to ethical issues. We informed the client upfront that we would not be telling him about all the daily activities of the car. He was paying us to recover his car, not to stalk someone.

A few weeks went by. The client told us that his lady friend would be coming over for several hours. (The GPS would have told us as much, but never mind.) Elrod found the car where she had parked it and went to work trying to start it. He was sweating but eventually the magic code worked. Per client instructions, he took it back to the dealership for safe-keeping, and we reported the good news to the client.

We thought it was mission accomplished. But people are funny. Men in love especially. A couple days later the client gave the car back to the lady friend. We didn't know what to think—all of our work, or rather Elrod's, for nothing. But, it was just another day. We can't control clients. In this case, we thought we should at least try to talk to him man-to-man to get him to reconsider his relationship with this woman. He later thanked us for our guidance and counseling.

Nearly the exact scenario had occurred 14 years ago, when an old guy hired me to repossess his car from the buxom young lady to whom he had given it. (He had also bought her a pair of luscious synthetic breasts, but he did not have any plans to deflate and repossess this gift.) Another May-December "romance"; the couple had broken up, and the sugar daddy moved to Idaho. He flew into Oakland late at night and would have to fly home early the next morning to feed his German Shepherds. He got off the plane in a wheelchair, and I got him into a rental car using his walker.

We went to her neighborhood in a working class block off San Pablo Avenue on the Berkeley-Oakland border. We waited until 2 a.m., then I went to work. I took the extra set of keys and walked over to the sedan. I could hear my heart coming out of my throat but managed to start the car and drive away. Ever the paranoiac, I wore gloves so as not to leave fingerprints in case the whole job somehow soured. The client drove the rental car to meet me in my neighborhood, and we packed up his gal's belongings and stuck them in a box that he would mail to her. He had someone coming in the morning who would take the car down to Long Beach to sell it.

He called me five hours later. He couldn't go through with it because she had called him to report the car stolen. He sang like a canary to baby-doll, promising her he would return the car. That Sunday morning I stuffed my bicycle into the back seat and brought the car back to her. I hoped I could just leave it at the curb and escape unnoticed, but she was waiting for me. As I pedaled away on my bicycle, a stacked blonde chased after me on foot, throwing cans and bottles. Don't get mad at me, toots! I was only doing a job for your geezer ex-lover.

* * *

The two cases I just discussed involved men wanting actual relationships with women. Sure, sex is a big part of this want, but those two seemed to want love more than carnal delights. As the case I am about to recount shows, however, the sex drive in some cheating men is unbridled. They will do anything for their fix: ruin marriages, blow through money, and destroy their own families. As the saying goes, they are thinking more with the small head than the big one.

For this case, my former assistant out of UC-Berkeley, Cornelius, joined me on a domestic that turned out to be one of my most lurid cheating-man probes. We ended up at a beach parking lot, Cornelius facing one side of the subject's truck with his video camera, while I took the other side with my camera. Each video showed the truck rocking while parked. Subsequent footage showed a man—our subject—and a woman emerging from the opposite backseat doors; my video showed the man tucking in his pants, and Cornelius's video had the woman straightening her blouse. We had nailed the subject for cheating, caught red-handed. We are not talking young love but two middle-aged people, lothario and seductress. They were co-workers. I'm not completely sure, but the woman he was cheating with also might have been married.

Funny enough, we had already caught the same man on a previous occasion, but the client wanted more proof. I never know exactly what a client makes of the evidence we give them, but some apparently are in denial. Several times we waited for him at his workplace and followed him and the female colleague to various locations. Because I had been out on him several times, my instinct told me that the day was coming when I would be "picked" or "made." These misgivings led me to rent a car for the assignment. I assumed the lead with Cornelius following in his car. After collecting that great footage at the beach we kept following him, at his wife's orders.

You can tell when you are about to be detected. The person you follow starts playing games, checking their mirrors and changing lanes to watch if you will change lanes. I knew one surveillance was over when I returned to my parked car after following a man on foot and found a wad of chewing gum on my door handle, no doubt placed there by the subject. My associate Al told me about an instance he knew he had been caught, when his subject paid his toll for him as she went through the Bay Bridge toll lanes just ahead of him.

The biggest myth of surveillance in a car is that it can be performed from a distance, as it's done in the movies. Wrong. In urban traffic you have to plaster yourself to your quarry's bumper –one stoplight missed or one right-on-red you can't keep up with spells disaster. Movies and TV make surveillance look far too casual and easy. People who are up to something are even tougher to follow. They know they are doing something bad and are literally looking over their shoulders. It's what lawyers call "consciousness of guilt."

After that day at the beach with Cornelius I sensed the end of the case. We got to the intersection at Piedmont and Macarthur in Oakland, and the subject came after me in his truck. I had been behind him, but he pulled over to let me go ahead and started chasing me. He flipped me off, frothing at the mouth behind the wheel. I had the rental car partly so that he could not identify me if he remembered my plate and had it run. (For this reason I never register my cars at my home address.) We ripped through the crowded Oakland streets at 60 mph until I lost him. Compared to a movie chase scene it seemed lame, but still I burned some rubber and slalomed through cars in traffic. Cornelius watched us from a distance, probably laughing his ass off. As in most cases, I have no idea how it ultimately ended for my client and her man, whether they patched up or broke up. It's always onto the next case. (As for Cornelius, he later got a job with the State Department for several years and now lives in Germany.)

CHAPTER 10

THE TRUTH ABOUT SURVEILLANCE: I DON'T PEE IN MY CAR

A FEMALE CLIENT HAD BROKEN UP WITH HER PARTNER, the father of their young son. He swore to her that there was no other woman. I went out to his place for six nights and saw no activity. One night she had me follow him after he dropped the child off at her place. I knew something was up because he drove on side streets at 50 mph. I stayed with him until he entered a parking lot in San Leandro, just south of Oakland. The client had informed me that he was vegetarian and didn't eat meat, yet his car was parked next to a Burger King. I hadn't seen him exit the car. Scanning the vicinity, I noticed a sushi restaurant. Maybe he was a pescetarian?

I went into the sushi place and saw him having dinner with a woman. Normally I would not immediately tell a client that I have caught the subject, but I trusted my client and called her. She said that she was on her way because she had to see it with her own eyes. I saw her park her car and go into the restaurant. While she was inside, my heart was in my throat not knowing what was happening. I envisioned tabloid headlines: "Three Dead in San Leandro Sushi Slayings." After three minutes, the client came out looking relieved and thanked me, saying that she simply had to see them together with her own eyes to prove to herself that it was real. Not a drop of blood on anyone.

I bring up this case to show how persistent you have to be about surveillance. I can't control the actions of the people I'm following. Clients are usually right when they suspect cheating. The good clients understand the whims of human behavior and surveillance. They know that they will maybe have to expand their budget to get results.

Surveillance is not exciting—some refer to it as "staring at garage doors." On the other hand, there is a certain Zen to it, especially if you have a lookout point where neighbors won't be up in your face every 20 minutes. When I take on a surveillance, I strive to be relaxed but focused. I try to maintain calm, while being aware that at any second I could see my subject and have to drive off. Other times, neighbors will notice a strange man in a strange car parked near their house. My rule is: lie to everyone except the cops. Often, we will call a local police dispatch to notify them we are doing a surveillance in order to pre-empt cops from rolling up on us and blowing our cover. (Of course I never tell dispatch who it is I have under watch or why.) I keep calm in the car by listening to my beloved Oakland A's on the radio, if I have a surveillance during baseball season. I probably listen to too much sports talk, but all-news is so damn repetitive, NPR too white, and political radio too predictable. I need to discover more podcasts and audio books because both would be perfect for occupying my fidgety mind.

Domestic cases and surveillance are also instinctive, although based on experience. Many times I am doing the work myself or a single operative is working a case for me. You have to scout out the area and look for entrances and exits. Are they most likely to be on foot or will they go to their car? What if you have three potential exits where the person could leave on foot? You make your best guess and have to trust yourself. When I do surveillance I like to think of my past victories and replay a "greatest hits" mental montage to boost my confidence. In all my years in the job, I have learned this about domestics and perhaps more broadly about surveillance:

- Have good information up front about your subject. We need a good starting address, descriptions, license plates, addresses they might frequent, detailed vehicle descriptions, etc.
- Surveillance is a lot like hunting or fishing. Don't expect instant results. If you stick to it day after day you will catch a fish. The worst thing you can do is be too aggressive in the beginning, which will get you detected.
- Police use numerous personnel and multiple vehicles on surveillance. We do it on an extremely low budget. Using two investigators might cost a bit more, but it's worth it because you can rotate cars, etc. On a solo surveillance, what can you do if the subject parks and walks away before you can find a parking space?

- This is not the movies. Following from a distance might work in Hollywood but not so much in a busy urban area. We have to follow closely, and yet we do lose subjects from time to time.
- The key is to get on a subject when he's outside his immediate area. At home I look out my door and know every car that belongs on my street. But once I'm on a main street, I have no idea who is in a car; the same goes for the subject you are following.
- Blend in. Use a vehicle that's appropriate. In the spiffy suburbs don't drive a '75 Dodge Dart. Maintain your car and its lights in good condition. Keep a full tank of gas because you don't know what will happen.
- Don't wear a clown suit to a funeral. Dress the part. You might need a couple different looks but don't ever dress in a way that will call attention to yourself. Stick to an anonymous look, as I do, and it works well.
- Nothing is better on a surveillance than a man-woman team. Lone man in car equals stranger danger. Lone man in car near any school equals call the cops!
- Eyes up! You are like a lifeguard scanning the horizon. You can't do the job with eyes down playing Candy Crush or nose-deep in Facebook on your iPhone. As a corollary to Murphy's Law, the second you avert your eyes is when your subject moves.

Surveillance focuses on vehicles and people. The biggest identifier on a vehicle is its license plate. I'm so obsessed with reading plates for a living that when I walk the dog around the block or simply drive to the grocery store I find myself looking at plates, practicing at memorizing them. Most investigators who do surveillance develop a skill for recognizing vehicle makes and models. God bless the surveillance subject who plasters political or sports team decals on rear windows and bumpers. They just made my job so much easier. Conversely, there is nothing worse than following a silver Camry or Accord or a black SUV in an upscale suburb. At night, I have to discover and focus on a unique feature of the vehicle's taillights.

For surveillance, I've used my 1999 blue Toyota Camry for the last few years. It's a grandma or grandpa ride, utterly non-descript. No bumper stickers or other identifiers on it. This car works much better for funkier places like Oakland and San Francisco than in the upscale suburbs, where anyone with a crappy car is assumed to be domestic help. Speaking of non-descript, check my wardrobe. I have a closet full of pants and sweaters in navy blue, gray, and black. I wear solid, boring colors so I don't call attention to myself. Surveillance is not about being invisible—it's about blending. I have always been good at not calling attention to myself. People would have a hard time picking me out of a lineup. "What did he look like?" "You know, white guy, middle-aged, not tall, not short, average."

I'm an average looking guy tailing regular people. For the most part the subjects we follow lean more toward working stiff than trust funder. Whereas on a legal case I put attorney name, client name and date on the case folder, on a privately retained surveillance case, I label the folder after the city or occupation or hobby of the subject to remind myself at a glance of a potential distinguishing feature. I suppose I have "plumber," "Raiders fan," and "baseball coach" somewhere in the archives. In one case, the subject appears in a photo flanked by two parrots. I labeled the file—you guessed it—"Parrot Man."

Most surveillance matters take me to parking lots. Tons of stuff goes down in parking lots. We follow people to them, watch them hump in them (if we are lucky), but mostly just sit in them until our asses go numb. There is nothing fun about a parking lot.

When it does come to a chase on a surveillance, we sometimes have to run red lights to stay with our subject. I hate doing this, but I hate admitting defeat just as much. If I think I have to run a light, I ask: 1) am I a danger to myself and to others, and 2) do I see any cops? In traffic I like to have a cover of one or two cars between myself and the target vehicle. I will stay to one side or the other so the driver can't get a good look at me in both his rearview and side view mirrors.

Food preference on surveillance? Nothing heavy. Credo from my wrestling days: a hungry wolf fights better. Watch the intake of liquids (including coffee), but stay hydrated, especially if the temperature is on the warm side. Beware the caffeine monster: a jittery shamus does not make the best decisions. I like Jolly Ranchers, Starbursts, a little bit of sugar free gum, nuts and trailmix. Sunflower seeds are fine but messy.

Still, I will only go so far in what I will do. I refuse to piss in my car. I will risk a run to the woods or to the closest Starbucks or Chevron rather than pee into a Gatorade bottle. What happens if you get startled or don't aim straight while going into the bottle? Ick.

The focus of growing my business and getting better at my business is a plan to make sure that I am not the guy in the parking lot for the next 22 years! I can just picture myself at age 70 in my Volvo with my high-powered binoculars and hearing aid on surveillance. If I keep doing surveillance into old age, I'm going to have to rely more on GPS devices.

GPS is the best thing to happen to the private dick since the trench coat. Law enforcement in California cannot use a GPS without a warrant on suspected criminal matters, and their use remains in something of a gray area in terms of legality. In our domestic and civil cases, however, we are allowed to use a GPS device as long as the client's name is on title and registration to the vehicle—I know this is riding a fine line but nothing in California penal code prohibits a person from using GPS on their own car. When I have a client who owns the car we are going to follow, I have them sign an agreement authorizing us to install the device. And if their spouse happens to be in the car without knowledge of the GPS, so be it. Additionally, many families have the phone locate service; some spouses use it to track their kids or partners, knowledge that can be passed on to us investigators in order to track the subjects. I don't take domestic assignments in routine boyfriend-girlfriend relationships where the couple has not been together for a long time. If I'm going to take the case, I want something to be at stake; they should have lived together for several years, for example. In the end, GPS technology is a huge cheat. It saves clients time and money because the investigator doesn't have to go out the door doing costly fieldwork. As powerful a tool as GPS may be, I still have to see with my own eyes what the subjects are doing. A GPS might tell me where a car is and has been but it provides no nuance or context about the people involved or their activity.

One domestic case in particular serves as an illustration of how GPS has changed the game. It took my eyes, ears, and video camera to document what the GPS signal led me to, but only after the GPS had provided the major intelligence. I was working for a man who suspected his wife of cheating with their child's basketball coach. I knew we were close because I had done surveillance on them at a church parking lot where they were hanging out together late at night after practice ended. The only problem was they were on the side of her vehicle where I could not get my camera on both of them or clearly see what they were doing. I had to call it a night.

Later I started reviewing the GPS data from the device we had installed on the vehicle owned jointly by the client and his wife. And wouldn't you know it, but it showed the car repeatedly turning up some remote road and stopping for about an hour each time at the same place. GPS does not give perfect locations, so I had to go out into the field to physically search for them. I found them in a parking lot in a wooded county park in an isolated area. If I had tried to enter the parking lot with my car, they would have heard crunching gravel or spotted me in an instant, so I parked some distance away and took video of her car then coach's car right alongside it.

Next I went in on foot and finally belly-crawled to obtain better footage. When in doubt, go to the high ground. Up a hill I went. But I still couldn't get great video because of the canopy of the larger trees. Over several days I tracked them to the same spot during what the GPS indicated was their regular meeting time. Each day it reached about 95 degrees as the June sun climbed higher in the sky, while I posted my video camera up on a tripod set to auto-record while I slithered and crawled through grass filled with ticks and insects, looking for a better vantage point. I reported back to the client with all my observations—I could even hear her moans in the back of her SUV—but I couldn't get any up-close footage of him exiting her SUV. The client wanted more and more detailed video, but I could only tell him that it was impossible due to the trees and secluded nature of their parking spots. I'm not sure how it ended. Sometimes we can only do so much. I felt that the evidence I was able to collect spoke for itself: three times I had obtained footage of their vehicles together, in the middle of the day, in a secluded spot. I doubt they were there to discuss the latest *Mad Men* episode.

As proven by the case of the parking-lot lovers, lines of sight and vantage points are important in surveillance. Sometimes leafy trees and big vehicles block my view and obscure the video. If the subjects are in a car parked parallel on a street, you can't be directly behind them because you can't get clear video. You also can't be right on top of them, because it's too noticeable. When you hold the video camera close to your eye, you don't want bystanders noticing you either because they could cause a commotion and blow it for you. Getting good video is trickier than one might think. I recommend to trainees that they go to the video camera only when they know it will give them clear footage of the subject.

The iPhone and other camera phones supplement the traditional, larger camcorders of private eyes. A smartphone has the advantage of not arousing suspicions: it allows you to take pictures of license plates or people from up close without shouting to the world that you are taking photos or video. Another, indirect advantage smartphones have given private eyes is that people using and playing on their phones become completely unobservant. Their heads and eyes are down, and I could sprint circles around them in a gorilla suit and they wouldn't even know it.

Even more discrete than the smart phone is a keychain video camera I use for filming indoors or to get close-up footage. The camera is concealed inside plastic casing of what looks to be an electronic car key. But like most cameras in any form, a keychain camera needs enough natural light to produce good video. In one case I had tracked a client's husband into the Mitchell Brothers O'Farrell Theater, a notorious pornographic theater and strip club in San Francisco's Tenderloin neighborhood. I saw him lurking next to the stage before going off to a private room with a saucy dancer. I thought I might have a chance at decent footage, but Mitchell Brothers keeps the place so dark that the camera could not pick up any facial features.

Camera or video use in any form comes only after a judgment of where the person will drive next and where you will need to position your vehicle. You must constantly evaluate likely exits and entrances, by vehicle and by foot. I just had one surveillance where the subject got a parking spot and was away on foot before I could find him. My assistant and I should have just parked immediately and run to cover the stairwells and elevators on each side. However, we were in separate vehicles so neither of us got a prime parking spot for watching and then following him.

Fortunately, we are always one phone call away from the next case that will allow us to use all our skills, experience, and technology.

Another successful outcome on a case involving GPS involved a client who feared that her husband had relapsed to an old pattern of drinking. He worked as an executive for a pharmaceutical company. They had a troubled marriage and were going to counseling, but she felt he was not being honest in therapy about his substance-abuse problems. She suspected drinking; he been in a serious auto accident many years ago and was drinking heavily at the time. I did surveillance without GPS a couple times, following him home on the back streets after he left work. I had an idea of which side street he was going to just before going home but had yet to see where he was parking.

One day the client contacted me while her husband was out at a baseball game. I had a window of a couple hours to meet with her and get a GPS installed on their car. Partner Elrod had extolled the virtue of double-sided Velcro for affixing a GPS to a car, but you need to make sure you have a clean metal surface free of oil and grease. I used a battery-powered GPS that holds a charge for about six days.

Over the next couple days I monitored the subject on the computer without following him in my car. I saw a pattern. He kept going to the same strip mall at about the same time each day after work. This was the most the GPS alone could tell me: he might have been hitting a Baskin Robbins, or a massage parlor across the street, or a sex toy store in equal likelihood. It was up to me to establish the context; still, now I knew where to look for him, and I wouldn't have to glue myself to his bumper as he left his workplace. I waited for him at the strip mall and three times filmed him entering a liquor store, buying cheap vodka, pounding the pint in his car, and driving home. I even retrieved the empty pint, still in the paper bag, out of the garbage can, just in case the client wanted physical evidence to confront him with.

Do I feel badly about violating his privacy or catching him? No, not really. He was engaging in this activity in plain view and in public. And after all, I need to make money. We are paid by clients to get information, we do our job well and we do it legally. No wonder the client couldn't progress with her husband in counseling; he was likely under the influence during the sessions.

For the investigator, surveillance is an odd combination of 95 percent boredom and 5 percent terror or excitement. My most vivid case memories are about surveillance. And the most vivid surveillance capers involve cheating spouse investigations.

A few highlights:

THE CASE OF THE MISSING VIAGRA

An Australian businessman came to San Francisco for more than a business trip. The wife back in Oz called me because she had counted his boner pills and found he was one pill short. My buddy Ed Crame and I staked out his Union Square hotel. All we had was a photo, but one afternoon we spotted him arm-in-arm with a young Chinese woman who towered above him in her stripper heels. They made for great video as he grabbed-ass over her chinchilla coat. They nuzzled. We filmed from opposite sides of the street. I eventually tracked Missy to a mansion near Los Altos Hills and learned she was an escort.

THE THREE-TIMING OPHTHALMOLOGIST

A young woman hired me to check out the eye doctor she was dating. Not only was he married but surveillance proved that he had another girlfriend on the side. The client was third in line!

I MARRIED A FAKE FIRE CAPTAIN
(AND I'M HAVING HIS BABY)

A nice woman in Walnut Creek was having doubts about her husband. Every day he dressed in his firefighter uniform and went off to work in San Francisco. The part about crossing the Bay Bridge on his commute to work in San Francisco held water, and his uniform turned out to be integral to his work, but I suppose it depends how you define work. As I discovered, he was approaching medical supply companies in the guise of a fire captain, shaking them down for CPR and other equipment needed by his department, and then selling it elsewhere and pocketing the proceeds. I think what had tipped her off was finding a dry cleaning receipt for one of his uniforms that showed he was paying out of pocket instead of it being a work expense. She took the news in stride; clearly she already knew he was some sort of fraud, but not the extent. She was about eight months pregnant; as in most of my cases, I don't know how it turned out.

VENTURE CAPITAL WEASEL

This case fills me with pride for the tail job I did in my four-cylinder Civic following a Porsche at more than 100 mph from Menlo Park through San Francisco. A pretty Japanese lady came to me with a story of betrayal. I instantly believed her—how could someone walk out on such a babe? She had been living with a British guy who worked on Sand Hill in Menlo Park, about 30 miles south of San Francisco. One day she came home from the gym, and he had just completely moved out, leaving the place as barren as Whoville after the Grinch had his way. She also learned about the same time that she was pregnant. She wanted to know his whereabouts and if there was another woman.

Enter our hero: Michael J. Spencer, Private Dick! I staked out his workplace. Guess where I waited for him? Bingo: the parking lot. He wore a suit and drove a new black Porsche. I wore jeans and drove a shitty white Honda Civic. Off he went north on 101 at about 4 p.m., just before rush hour. He cranked it up to over 100 mph, not because he knew I was on him, but because he had a Porsche. I stuck with him all the way through San Francisco. I even got out and watched him shop at Whole Paycheck. (What, did you think he was going to Safeway?) Next came the hard part: following him down side streets in San Francisco until he stopped and went into a high rise. Over the next week or so I confirmed that he was living there and confirmed that he lived with another woman. I gave the information to my client. She didn't seem too upset, but at least she had some answers. And again, I never knew how it ended.

PROFESSIONAL ATHLETES

I have had a few cases with female clients either engaged or married to professional athletes. One such client was engaged to a pro football player. She had a nursing degree and an excellent education and background. Her boyfriend gave her a disease after having sex with a stripper during training camp. She stayed with him even after the VD incident; questions about his commitment obviously lingered. She had me follow him to a hotel where he was meeting an old flame. I almost knocked on his hotel room door because I had lost sight of him with the other woman in the hotel lobby. Turned out he was still in the lobby with the other woman, and I never saw them sneak off together. I'm not sure, but I think the client and her football player ended up getting married.

THE BANKER SHAKEDOWN

In the late '90s an Oakland woman contacted me with an unusual request: she wanted me to hide in her closet and surreptitiously tape her doing it with her older boyfriend. My answer was no. I asked, "Why would you want me to do that?"

"He's married, and I want to show his wife that he's with me for good." I thought of a compromise. I would agree to film them out on a date, holding hands, etc., a PG-13 version. Still, I thought it pretty damn strange. I had her pick a spot on Piedmont Avenue in Oakland with big plate-glass windows where I could easily film them from the passenger seat of my car. I did the job, turned over the tape, and the matter was closed.

Four years later, an investigator for the federal public defender's office called me to ask if I knew anything about a certain woman. Of course, her name alone didn't jog my memory, so I asked him about the circumstances. Uh-oh. Her "boyfriend" was a banking executive, and she now stood accused of blackmailing him. I told the investigator what I knew and never had to appear in court or testify. I've since become more seasoned at sizing up my clientele.

Now you know what goes on in stakeouts and surveillance. But most of my money I make through serving personal injury and criminal defense attorneys. In that sense, it might be more accurate to call myself a "legal investigator" than a private investigator.

CHAPTER 11

WALKING IS DANGEROUS— PERSONAL INJURY AND WRONGFUL DEATH CASES

O N A BRIGHT SAN FRANCISCO MORNING in 2009 an elderly Chinese lady was making her way across the street. She took three or four steps before a garbage truck struck her and dragged her down Polk Street under its back right tire for another 20 feet before stopping.

The incident occurred at about 9 a.m. on the edges of San Francisco's Tenderloin, a neighborhood known for its homeless, prostitutes, hustlers, urine odors, and filth. It's a place where living is hard and dying is mean. But that day it was one of the Tenderloin's denizens who proved to be the hero for the 75-year-old grandmother.

Two to three people a day are hit by vehicles in San Francisco. The city ranks first in the United States for pedestrians and cyclists killed or injured by motor vehicles. According to the *San Francisco Chronicle*, more than 800 pedestrians were injured in 2009. The city averages about 17 pedestrian deaths a year—an astounding number, which nevertheless signifies good business for plaintiffs' lawyers, for insurance defense law firms, and for various experts and private investigators working for either side. In a routine arrangement, a plaintiff's attorney takes 33 percent of a case upon settlement. Of course, these lawyers have expenses to cover while the case advances, and they also risk the possibility of losing costs and everything at trial. (In my many years as a private investigator, most good attorneys do not gamble on iffy cases. They put the money into an investigation and don't pursue frivolous cases.)

The lady run over on Polk Street nearly died. She suffered a broken pelvis and numerous catastrophic injuries. She is the mother of five and a grandmother of 10. She will need medical care the rest of her life. The collision and subsequent dragging left her blood and skin on the pavement.

I admit to having a pro-lawyer bias, which should come as no surprise given the fact that I'm making a living from trial lawyers. That being said, lawyers get a bad name as bottom feeders, ambulance chasers, etc. We've all heard the jokes or the misinformation about the McDonald's coffee case or the endless cries for "tort reform." As in any profession, there are good lawyers and there are bad.

The best lawyers go in guns blazing when they think they might have a good case. They prepare every case as though it's going to trial and on the assumption that they are going to win in court. If nothing else, going scorched earth in the beginning digs up all the relevant facts, so that you beat your opponents, an insurance defense firm, to the punch. You land a lot of body shots, and eventually you just overwhelm your foe.

Maybe from the lurid stories I've recounted in previous chapters, you might get the impression that I'm just waiting around for the phone to ring, beckoning me with tales of weirdness and big money. You would be wrong. Day in, day out, I am in the trenches digging for information and advancing a legal case. Whether it's a pedestrian injury, or a pedestrian versus auto, or bike versus pedestrian, my bread-and-butter tends to be helping victims injured due to negligence or something worse.

In the San Francisco case of the woman hit by the garbage truck, the attorneys contacted me fairly soon after the incident to investigate. They are an excellent law firm with a record of success in personal injury and other cases. They knew they had a potentially big case and weren't hesitant to spend the time and money to build their case against the truck operator as well as the owner of the collection company providing sanitation and recycling services to the city. Time is critical in any investigation. I have found that once you get beyond three months or so after an incident, memories really start to fade. Most of us can't remember what we had for breakfast yesterday.

I like to work for plaintiffs' attorneys because they typically get the case first, which means I am the first to meet the witnesses, giving me the chance to build a rapport with them. Just like the police, I aim to lock a witness into a statement. I prefer to audio-record them, with their permission of course, which comes in handy for the attorney when and if they have to depose the witness. A deposition is merely a more formal interview with attorneys from each side asking questions.

Building an early rapport with a witness provides a huge advantage. By the time the second or third or fourth investigator approaches a witness, they tend to bristle. I call it "witness fatigue." No one likes answering the same questions over and over, taking the time to repeat the whole ordeal, or recalling a traumatic event. I try to be friendly, honest, patient, and firm with each witness. My days as a newspaper reporter come in handy: a good interviewer trades information and allows the subject the opportunity to express himself or herself. I only try to keep them on track or more or less on topic.

My first task is a thorough reading of the police report, paying close attention to the accounts of all parties involved including the witnesses. In the case of the woman injured on Polk Street, two issues loomed large: was she definitely in the crosswalk when struck, and who had the light? The claim would be badly damaged if it turned out she had been walking on a red light or was outside the crosswalk. In that case, I suppose some recovery might have been possible, but the defense attorney could "apportion" most of the blame to her if she was found to be jaywalking.

The police report had a handful of witnesses, none of whom would I recall as rock solid solely on the basis of a reading of the report. Police at a scene, maybe even more so than journalists, write under extreme deadline pressure. They are already going from call to call and try to do their best. Still, directions can get changed, speeds recorded incorrectly, and facts transposed. Knowing this, when I interview witnesses I try not to rely too much on a police report so as not to bias myself before each interview.

From the police report, I identified one witness—"Larry Jones"—as a priority. He had been first on the scene and had witnessed the entire incident, and had even yelled at the truck driver to stop. Although the police report referred to Larry as homeless, it did have an address for him, which turned out to be a liquor store three blocks from the scene.

Another potential witness had been a pedestrian walking south on Polk who had heard the commotion and looked behind him to see the truck and the victim.

Next? The man who saw part of the accident from across the street as he was on his way to his job at a coffee shop. Finally, the barista's buddy who was walking with him but was not mentioned in the police report. Barista buddy proved tantalizing but barren in usefulness as a witness.

The liquor store cashed various assistance checks for its clients. "He comes here every few days," a clerk said of Larry. "He sleeps around here at night and brings us his checks." It took a few days, but one Saturday morning, I found Larry. He was a skinny African American man in his late 50s. He stumbled a little over his words but could carry a conversation. As we walked towards the scene, he recounted his life story: he had grown up in the Hudson River Valley, served in the Army, lived in Texas or Oklahoma for a while, and wound up in San Francisco.

Larry agreed to give a recorded statement at the intersection—the scene. He indicated that the woman had not been very far out into the crosswalk when the truck just rolled over her with its rear tire. He stated three times that the woman had the green light to walk across. He broke out in tears recalling how he had slammed his fists on the side of the truck to get the driver to stop. He pointed to the spot on the pavement where her body had come to rest and where her blood and skin left a trail. I had him sketch the positions of the victim and the truck during the incident and had him sign the paper.

I telephoned the other pedestrian witness, the one who had been walking south on Polk. Nice guy, stable, Mr. Normal. He came to the scene and recalled the sequence: he had had a green light walking south on Polk but it had turned yellow as he was halfway across, obliging him to speed-walk to make it in time. This fact jumped out at me: if he had barely made it across before the southbound light turned red, and he had then walked 10 yards further before hearing the noise of the accident behind him, it meant that the eastbound garbage truck must have had a red light and the pedestrian a green light.

The barista claimed not to remember much of the accident and could not recall whether the victim had the green light. He explained that his view had been blocked, and added that I could check with his friend who was near him. I dubbed this potential witness the Sensitive Artist. I got his phone number but he wouldn't return my calls. The attorney wanted this guy bad, so I went into hound-mode for him. The Barista confirmed that his sensitive buddy had freaked out over the gruesome accident he had witnessed.

I tracked him to one apartment in San Francisco, but he had already moved out. I learned he had a record of arrests for public intoxication in his hometown in Orange County. Through additional research of social media and Facebook, I learned he was a singer-songwriter and played at various places in San Francisco. I sent him messages, but he never took the bait. One night I saw that he would be performing at a laundromat south of Market Street. I went with my wife to look for him, letting her try to make the contact. He froze when she mentioned that I wanted to talk to him about the accident. He pretty much said, "fuck you"; we decided to avoid him for now but keep him in mind for a subpoena if he became essential. (Attorneys don't want to deal with an overtly hostile witness.)

A couple months went by. As a private investigator I hustle and work on multiple cases simultaneously. Legal cases take time. In the meantime, I hung flyers looking for other potential witnesses, ordered 911 tapes from the police, and did a surveillance assignment for the case.

The attorney had me do a background on the truck driver. He turned out to have one previous violation on his driving record. The attorney asked me to stake out the intersection at the same time and route to observe whether the truck usually stopped for red lights or just rolled through them on the red without looking. Sitting deep down in my car seat, I poked my head and video camera up to record the truck. Sure enough, the truck rolled the red light without stopping while turning. It was easy to see how the accident had likely occurred: driver is up high in his seat on the left side heading downhill and to the right; short woman is out in the crosswalk on his right side, in his blind spot. He likely never saw her and stopped only because Larry was screaming and banging on the side of the truck. For her part, she possibly never saw the truck coming up on her. Catastrophic incidents occur when two parties don't see each other at exactly the same time. I don't like to use the term "accident," which implies no one is at fault.

Five months had passed since I began work on the case. Word from the attorney was that the truck driver's employer was digging in his heels and would fight hard against any charges. The attorney knew a deposition loomed for Larry. I started loose inquiries for Larry to make sure he was still in touch with the liquor store and cashing his assistance checks there. We now had a deposition date and time at the law office: 9 a.m. My job was to: a) find Larry, b) keep him sober, c) dress him in some nice clothes, and d) transport him to the deposition. The night before the deposition I found him in an alley and told him I would be by at 6:30 a.m. to go get some breakfast with him. It was ethically okay to buy him a meal or two, but we weren't permitted to pay him more than the standard $45 witness fee.

Larry brought a wingman with him to breakfast that morning who promised to "help keep him calm" before the deposition. If he was good for Larry, I wasn't going to get rid of him. We all three had breakfast together at McDonald's. I felt pretty good about Larry's mood and demeanor. (I would later learn from the attorney that Larry had downed a pint of whatever liquor earlier that morning before I started with him, but with the meal and the passing of several hours he had sobered up.) I gave Larry some pants and a dress shirt I had bought for him at The Gap. We arrived at the law office at Union Square in San Francisco around 9:30 a.m. The receptionist did a double take at the sight of the clean-cut investigator with the two homeless men. Larry disappeared into a conference room where four lawyers were waiting for him. I thought it would be best if Wingman and I went outside to wait until the deposition ended.

About every hour I walked back up to the law office to check on Larry but he was still being deposed. After about three and half hours the attorney called: Larry was done. The attorney told me that Larry's account during the deposition was consistent with what he had told me in his statement. Under questioning from the lawyers, he would not be shaken from his conviction that the elderly victim had been inside the crosswalk and had a green light when struck and dragged almost to death. I enjoyed the ride back to the liquor store with Larry and Wingman.

The case settled for $5 million; of that, the attorneys for the victim made about $1.3 million while the star witness got an Egg McMuffin Meal Deal and $45 in cash. (I made about $2,000 for my legwork.) Ethically, you simply can't pay witnesses big money for their testimony—it would only be incentive to lie. Fair? Maybe not, but anyone in that situation would hope someone like Larry would step up and do the right thing. As with most of my cases, I haven't kept up on how the victim is doing. I'm sure she still needs almost constant medical care, and the settlement amount seems right considering the trauma, damage, negligence, and so on.

I can only imagine that Larry, if he is still alive, is still out on the streets, sleeping in alleys and drinking to quell his mind and his pain. I should find him and bring him a meal. Larry is a hero.

I make money off tragedies. It wears on me, but I take some comfort if I can help a victim or their family in the process.

CHAPTER 12

FIGHTING INSURANCE COMPANIES
AFTER FATAL SHOOTINGS

O N A SATURDAY morning in 1996 I sat in my cruddy apartment on Martin Luther King Jr. Way in Oakland listening to the UC Berkeley student radio station. A mother poured out her story to a radio host. Her 18-year-old son had been shot and killed by a 24-year-old "friend" in a fit of jealousy after a party at the house. The killing had occurred in the home where the shooter lived with his parents. The shooter was described as reckless and had a history of gun incidents. The victim had had a promising future in college football and in general. The victim's mother was fighting for justice; although the 24-year old was facing criminal charges, she felt that not enough was being done to investigate the circumstances of her son's death.

The police had already completed the criminal investigation and charged the shooter. It seemed to me that the case had potential for a civil lawsuit. Certainly, the mother's sincerity and anguish touched me; I also saw that there was money to be made for an attorney and for me.

I called a criminal defense attorney I knew to be industrious: Bart Rothman of San Francisco. Bart is a bright lawyer with soul and humanity. He is primarily a criminal lawyer but has some experience doing civil cases. He is principled and a fighter, willing to slug it out with an insurance company and ready to bond with a client.

Bart advanced the theory that we should go after the homeowner's policy of the shooter's parents, given that they owned the house where the fatality had occurred. As a civil case, the standard of proof was different from the classic "beyond a reasonable doubt" required in a criminal case—a civil case requires only a "preponderance of evidence." (The O.J. Simpson trials illustrate the concept of criminal vs. civil trials—O.J. was found not guilty in the criminal trial, whereas in the civil trial he was found liable for the two deaths.) Nothing would bring back her beautiful 18-year-old son, but maybe the parents of the shooter could at least be taught a lesson. Why and how? We had to prove that the parents knew of the past gun incidents involving their son and that they had done nothing to stem the problems occurring on their property.

I do not that believe I violated any ethical standards or state codes by putting the potential client in touch with Rothman. I did not solicit her immediately after the incident, out in the street, or at a hospital or at some other venue or location where she might be in a vulnerable state. The attorney never directed me to contact her or any other potential clients. I was not even entirely sure whether she had a civil case. Moreover, the attorney paid me a straight hourly rate and not any sort of contingency. I simply believed that it would be good for her to talk to a civil lawyer; it would be her decision alone as to whether to bring a lawsuit.

I had my work cut out for me in determining whether there would be a winnable civil suit. I confirmed several past incidents of gun incidents on and off the property committed by the suspect, Tito Guerrero, along with his roommate at the house. The evidence was available in public records such as police reports, but the major factor was the statements provided by neighbors who had organized meetings about the situation prior to the murder and who had complained to the parents about loud parties and gunfire.

It's one thing to complain about things; it's another to willingly get involved in a legal case. This divide is precisely where a good investigator and attorney can make a difference in securing a case. On our side we had residents pissed off about a bad neighbor who never did anything to curtail a dangerous tenant—their son, the shooter. We were on the side of justice; our client had suffered a massive loss. When witnesses have told their story a couple times, they don't want to tell it a third and a fourth time. After the police and me, the next in line would be an insurance defense investigator hoping for scraps at best.

By the same token, it's human nature to avoid sticking your neck out. People don't want to put their name in a court record that implicates someone else. At this point, the criminal case had still not concluded. What if the suspect were exonerated and set free? If he heard that his neighbors had talked to a lawyer about him, wouldn't he want revenge?

All valid concerns. But Rothman and I knew that if we could get sworn statements and depositions from witnesses, the truth would come out, and the insurance company would be overwhelmed. We coaxed the leader of the neighborhood group, a mother of two young children, into giving statements and later a deposition against the parents/landlords. She was fed up with the gunfire across the street. The fatal shooting had been the fourth incident in two years involving guns at the house. We had her on record complaining to the shooter's parents and giving notice that their son and tenant was the problem. Once she went on record, others in the neighborhood fell into line.

Another aspect of the case was interviewing people who knew the victim personally and could testify that he had had a bright future ahead of him. I don't know exactly how courts calculate a dollar figure on loss of life but I assume it's a combination of age and potential. As I recall, the civil case settled for something near $1 million. The shooter was convicted and served 12 years in prison, which seems on the light side for taking a life. (I read later that the shooter after release had found work driving a truck for Goodwill; nowhere in the article did it mention him expressing remorse for what he had done.)

* * *

Many of my cases are just monumentally sad. I do the best I can do in the name of justice. In the context of this book, I have recounted these cases of wrongful death and premises liability—the cases that I still think about several years after they resolve or settle—in order to show that I do sink my teeth into serious matters. Many have the perception that private investigators are just goofing around in their cars, video camera in one hand and burger in the other. Maybe the talk of justice sounds schmaltzy or corny, but after a loved one's death, that's all the parents or next of kin have by way of consolation. And yes, I am getting paid, and so are the attorneys. On the other side of the coin, insurance company lawyers and insurance investigators make money defending claims, so I think we are all on even moral ground. I prefer working on the plaintiff's side, though I believe that I have the intellectual discipline not to bend or alter facts that don't support a client's case.

A couple of years ago I handled the case of a 20-year-old man, Jeremy Hansen, who was shot and killed while trying to break up a fight in the parking lot of Hernando's Cocktail Lounge in Hayward, a gritty, working-class suburb south of Oakland. By all accounts Hansen was a great young man, working and attending a community college, about to transfer to a university. His parents sued the bar, alleging negligent security and a host of other claims having to do with premises liability and negligence.

The story was that Hansen had been working in the bar as a DJ and was drinking there despite being underage. A fight had broken out inside the bar between two women; they were kicked out, but a crowd loitered at closing time. A friend of one of the girls started up the fight again in the parking lot. An altercation ensued between security and the girls and their boyfriends. At some point, young Mr. Hansen spotted a guy dragging a girl by her hair and tried to intervene. A bouncer also confronted the man and punched him. The man went to his car, retrieved a gun, and fired one shot into the air and another into the crowd, hitting Hansen. A few weeks later, Shawn Thomas was arrested and charged with the shooting; he eventually took a plea deal for voluntary manslaughter.

My partner Elrod and I met with Hansen's parents. A case becomes real when you meet the clients and feel their suffering and rage. The victim's dad cried upon remembering his son. The mother had the anger. I sat nodding and listening, as did Elrod. My partner has a gravitas about him beyond his years, perhaps acquired from his military combat experience. He knows grief and loss. We connect with our clients. I simply can't put into words the sadness of suffering parents. In the end, it is supreme motivation to go investigate and get justice.

I have enough experience to know what I have to do to prove a case. In the civil case for Hansen's parents, we would have to show that:
- The bar was serving under-aged customers
- The bar was employing security staff with minimal or improper training
- The fight that wound up in the parking lot had started in the bar
- Bar security had kicked the belligerents out of the bar but had done nothing to clear the parking lot
- The bar had a history of past incidents and violations

From police reports we had 40 potential witnesses to the incident. The police did arrest and charge Thomas in the death. A police report is useful in that it provides names, but it is often cursory and brief in that the police are trying to obtain information sufficient for an arrest, and nothing beyond that. It's up to me to develop witness information to support the civil suit. In such cases where the witnesses are many and disparate, I don't call in advance. For this one, Elrod and I spent many weekends cold-calling witnesses. I enjoy the dynamic of working with a partner. Interviews are spontaneous, and a good partner like Elrod brings up questions that would not occur to me. I can sit back and listen and take notes, or I can take the lead on the questioning. We found a few witnesses who recalled being served several times while underage because they knew people working at the bar or on security.

I found out that the lead security officer at the bar had prior convictions for violence; the night of the shooting he had been celebrating his birthday when the altercation started. I suspected he was drunk or drinking at the time. While many bars contract out to professional security staff, this bar hired its own staff and generally did not provide proper training for dealing with volatile and violent situations. When it came time to serve the lead security officer with deposition subpoenas, I found myself engaged in cat-and-mouse games. Finally, I served him in court when I knew he would be there for an unrelated family law matter. I waited in the hallway, made the identification on the basis of his photo, and served the papers. He was later found in contempt for not appearing for the deposition.

In these big cases, when I need an extra boost, I return my thoughts to the victim and his or her family. The memory of the crying dad and the angry mom in their living room provided me with all the motivation I would need. Additionally, my own insecurities push me in my work. What if I don't do a good job and the scummy bar doesn't have to pay a dime or face any penalties? What if the bar owners just don't give a shit about this young man? What if the client or family thinks I'm weak, and what if I fail? This self-questioning might seem excessive, but it motivates me to get results and to do the right thing.

We pursued the case in part because we recognized that the bar had inadequate security procedures in place. There is no reason to allow patrons to loiter outside the premises near and after closing time. Did the bouncer escalate the situation by punching the man who later returned with a gun? Had bar management known that Jeremy Hansen was a minor?

By gathering printouts of prior police responses at the bar and searching city planning records for other suits against the bar, I found what I needed to prove the case. I also obtained records of investigations conducted by the state Department of Alcoholic Beverage Control. Someone had sued the bar four years earlier after a patron had struck a man with his vehicle in the parking lot. The city had sent letters to the bar owners warning them to clean up their act and hire better security. In response, the bar owners essentially did nothing. Meanwhile, the bar's clientele had shifted to a more volatile customer base, whereas in years past it was strictly a neighborhood spot. (I learned this by interviewing three of the bar's previous owners.) Added to that was the fact provided to me in a statement by the property manager that prior to the shooting she had notified the bar that their lease would not be renewed, and that the other tenants had wanted them closed.

The attorney informed me that the insurance policy limit the bar carried was $1 million. The bar owners, a husband and wife, were stubborn, and their attorneys weren't going to offer a dime. I kept subpoenaing witnesses for depositions, until one day the attorney told me I could stop: with a trial on the horizon, the bar settled the case. I don't know the exact amount, but I assume it was for the policy limit. Ninety-five percent of cases resolve in a settlement, in what amounts to high-stakes poker.

Another memorable wrongful death investigation involved a valet from a national hotel chain who had shot and killed a patron in a dispute over a parking space at the hotel. My investigation would prove that the shooter had a history of on-the-job incidents, including verbal altercations with customers, while working at other hotels in the chain. Instead of firing the troubled employee, the hotel had simply moved him from a job in San Francisco to nearby San Mateo County. The hotel's lawyers apparently tried to argue that his behavior had occurred outside the scope of his employment. The argument apparently wasn't strong enough. I now see on the attorney's web site that the attorney settled the case with the hotel for $1.25 million.

* * *

A high proportion of fatal and serious incidents, especially those involving vehicles and pedestrians, occur at the exact split second when each party is not paying attention. The pedestrian has his head down to read an email, while the driver looks at the pretty girl on the sidewalk. The truck driver is backing up and can't see out of the side view mirror just as the warehouse worker's attention is distracted.

Although I'm not a scientist or engineer, a good deal of my work involves looking at why things happen and why things fail. I recall one case at Fisherman's Wharf in San Francisco where a metal pole on a bungee-type ride collapsed, striking and injuring several children. The attorneys sent me to videotape how the ride operators were handling the children. The ride was a sort of slingshot in which the kids would jump around in a swing over a trampoline surface. The swing was suspended from flexible cords attached to two tall metal poles anchored to the ground. Jumping straight up and down worked fine and did not pose any danger. The incident had occurred after the ride operators began pulling kids in the swing out to the side and launching them at angles. The metal pole failed to support the weight of the swing, bent, collapsed, and fell into a crowded pen where children were waiting for their turn. One of the injured children had been cut so deeply that his skull was visible through the wound. My video segments demonstrated that the ride operators were still pulling children out on angles to send them into the air. The case settled, but I have no idea of the amount.

In one case a malfunctioning automatic door at a large grocery store chain had closed prematurely on a patron, striking her in the head. The case involved videotaping hours and hours of footage of the door in action and looking over the footage for a faulty pattern. I've investigated trains striking pedestrians and tried to find factors that might have obscured the pedestrian's vision or hearing. I once even had a personal injury case involving dog shit. A lawn maintenance worker had complained to a homeowner to clean up after his or her pet. One day, as the man was working in the yard up on a ladder, the ladder slid in some dog poop, causing him to lose his balance, fall off, and shatter his knee. He lay in pain for about eight hours before someone found him. The homeowner's insurance company offered him nothing; the lawn worker's attorney went to trial and lost. I've handled more than a few scalding hot water cases where patrons were seriously burned by tea or coffee falling off a table from a lazy Susan–type device.

To put things in baseball language: good attorneys use me as a set-up man or late relief until the "closer" comes in to nail it. The closers would be the actual scientists, experts, and engineers who prepare diagrams and findings based on the evidence I've obtained in either witness statements or relevant documentary, audiovisual, or other material. Again, the good attorneys know how to prepare for trial and don't skimp on the resources required for working up a case. They have a system, and I'm a significant part of that system.

All of this experience in documenting the factors behind death and serious injury makes me see life events in terms of odds. I don't put too much stock in randomness or luck. Certain behaviors, risks, and habits greatly increase the chances of catastrophic injury. As you will read in the next chapter, one former client nearly paid with his life several times for his willingness to gamble.

CHAPTER 13

MR. CORVETTE MEETS
THE ULTIMATE FIGHTERS—
WHEN A CASE EXPLODES

NOT ALL CASES go so well for attorneys or for the private investigator.
Steve Khera and his date Renae had bopped into a Reno casino lobby at about 1 a.m. on a Saturday when a blond, muscular young man blurted out: "Hey, you look like a hooker!" Renae went to slap him, and he put her in an armbar, a wrestling move popularized by Ultimate Fighting Championship (UFC) fighter Ronda Rousey that can break the arm if deployed for an extended length of time. Khera threw a Nolan Ryan fastball with his cocktail glass, ricocheting off the assailant's head.

Bad move. For the next few minutes, with no hotel security in sight, the man hit by the cocktail glass and several of his large buddies proceeded to chase Khera around the hotel lobby until they got him on the floor. When Khera tried to defend himself with a stanchion, one or more of the men stomped him until they caved in his eye socket. Khera and his date flew home, where he was admitted to a hospital the next day.

How could you have a donnybrook in the lobby of a major hotel, on a weekend night no less, with no security in sight? Didn't the Atlantis like any other business have a duty to protect its customers?

These assailants weren't your ordinary street toughs. Khera and his date had the misfortune to run across some very violent and liquored-up Ultimate Fighters, including but not limited to Frank Shamrock and Jerry Bohlander of Lion's Den Mixed Martial Arts. Witnesses told me that the fighters had been upstairs at a bachelor party in an Atlantis nightclub, where they were grabbing women's asses and acting like jerks. Frank's brother is the even more notorious Ken Shamrock. (As I'm writing this, I've just noticed that Ken has omitted from his official bio the detail that in 1987 he faced a lawsuit in Reno alleging that he had stomped and beaten then–BYU football star Trevor Molini. Around that time Ken Shamrock relocated for martial arts training in Japan, where the civil judgment from the Molini case could not be enforced.) Bohlander, according to press reports, later became a Napa County sheriff's deputy who was involved in two fatal shootings on the job; both were ruled justified.

"You are only as good as your client," goes an adage about civil law. I learned that the hard way on this case. Along the trail, I chased after UFC fighters, drove all over Reno looking for witnesses, developed an affection for my deeply flawed client, had an awesome time, learned a lot, and, sadly, never saw a big payday on a case that once looked like gold.

I had known my client Steve Khera, legal name Khamiljit Singh Khera, for a couple years before I started working on his big civil case. He was the flamboyant manager of "Mr. Corvette," an auto dealership in Fremont, California, that staged promotional events featuring bikini babes parading out in front of the shop. We met on a criminal defense case for one of his bodyguards, arrested on a firearms violation at a San Francisco nightclub. I knew Khera was shady and figured he might be into loansharking or other forms of "collections." It seemed that there were always cops sniffing around his car dealership.

Khera called me one day in 1999 to say that he had just had the crap kicked out of him up at the Atlantis Hotel and Casino. He needed an attorney. I thought about it for a bit and took him to Eric Safire, a successful San Francisco attorney. We came up with a plan: Safire would pay my costs on the investigation, but I would only get paid for my time after a successful trial or settlement. I agreed to take the case on contingency—decent for attorneys but very bad for an investigator without deep pockets. Never take a case on contingency as a private eye; if it goes to court and you are called to testify, you will be portrayed as having a motive to lie or shade your testimony in order to win or to get paid. It's just all around bad for business. But, this was Reno. Why not gamble?

I felt like working in Reno on a serious injury case involving goons and a colorful client was in itself almost a form of payment. It was certainly a form of entertainment. Reno is Vegas's ugly trampy cousin to the north. It sits in a high desert at about 4,400 feet with snow-covered peaks up to 10,000 feet. Reno is just north of the world-famous vacation playground of Lake Tahoe. Though resorts are the order for Lake Tahoe,

Reno is a hard city with a few big casinos, lots of pawnshops, and cheap motels. "But I shot a man in Reno just to watch him die," as Johnny Cash sang, seems an apt description of the place. A stiff wind always howls through Reno. For what it's worth, I have flown out of Reno next to passengers barfing due to the windy turbulence.

The Atlantis sits on South Virginia Street several miles south of downtown Reno. It's in an isolated spot. Hotel cameras apparently captured footage of the van the fighters drove away in. The police finally got involved in the case, but no arrests were made because no witnesses would cooperate. I at least had the names of a few of the staffers at the Atlantis to go by. Several of them gave me recorded statements in which they acknowledged that while they had known the fighters were drinking and behaving like jerks, they had not bothered to remove them or keep them separate from other patrons.

We needed to partner with an attorney in Nevada, and I found the right one. I picked this lawyer because he had been successful in another "inadequate security" case against the Atlantis. Khera and I flew up to Reno so that I could start working on his case, chasing after witnesses. I toiled while Khera and his roll of $10,000 in cash worked the blackjack tables of Silver Legacy and the Peppermill.

Things looked peachy. There was no sense in chasing after the ultimate fighters as defendants because they did not have deep pockets and were continually on the move. Witnesses, however, were falling into place and giving me names of other witnesses. Safire and I sweated Khera about his own background, trying to make sure he didn't have too many skeletons in his closet that would make him seem unsympathetic to a jury or in a settlement. Khera disclosed a juvey robbery beef that he had beaten and some reckless driving stuff but nothing major, or so we thought.

I had done some of my best investigative work ever to make this case. I crisscrossed Washoe County and all parts of Reno finding witnesses and obtaining full, detailed recorded statements that would be turned into declarations for the witnesses to sign. I gave witnesses the movie line, "know anyone else who would know about this?" and sure enough they coughed up names of additional witnesses. I recall up to seven witnesses giving statements about the fighters' behavior at the bachelor party and the fact that nothing was done to control them. I did everything in my power to ensure a successful outcome for the client.

But like the dice hitting craps or that double down that loses to the dealer's six-card 21, the case against the Atlantis began to fizzle.

The first setback was the death, apparently by suicide, of the Nevada attorney. His death apparently had nothing to do with our case. I'm not sure but recall it might have been related to a serious medical condition. That meant we had to find and partner with another Nevada attorney. Meanwhile, I had racked up more than $20,000 in billable hours and was wondering if I would ever get paid. For most people, $20,000 is a big windfall; to a struggling private investigator, it's a fortune. It would have been enough money to pay off bills and take it easy for a couple months.

More bad news. Medical experts found that Khera had a pre-existing brain condition. The doctors said that if it weren't for the beating and resulting examination, his main injury would never have been detected. In essence, the fighters had done him a favor by smashing his eye-socket! (I had taken photos of Khera's wounds. Nasty. The whole side of his head had to be repaired and stapled shut.)

In 2003, with settlement talks looming, I got a call one day from Eric Safire with horrible news. The feds had just picked up Khera on several federal drug charges. Bye-bye, payday. The first words out of my mouth after hanging up with Safire were likely *Fuck! Fuck! Fuck!*, and I'm not one for swearing. If it had been a scene in a movie, we would have watched the Mike Spencer character paged by Safire, hearing the news in a phone booth, then smashing the phone receiver to pieces, kicking and punching nearby newspaper vending boxes, and finally passing out in a gutter surrounded by empty whiskey bottles. Lesson learned: I will never again take a case on contingency. Risky clients make for iffy paydays.

As for Khera, federal agents had raided his San Ramon home, where they found $35,000 in cash and several handguns. I had known that Khera really, really liked to gamble. Court documents show that over several years, Khera had become involved in dealing MDMA (ecstasy), pot, cocaine, and methamphetamines. I had known he liked to hustle, but *wow*. As it turned out, Khera was essentially a middleman in a drug organization. The court records noted a "sizable surgical scar" on the right side of his head from the beating at the Atlantis. Khera turned down the plea deals. He was found guilty and sentenced to 360 months

(30 years) in federal prison. While serving his sentence, a Sacramento County jailer wrote a letter of commendation to the federal court praising Khera for good behavior, such as translating Punjabi and alerting jail staff to a suicidal inmate.

Whereas Khera lived needing criminal defense attorneys, one client of mine tried to do everything right in life but still found himself on the wrong end of the law, as we will see.

CHAPTER 14

CRIMINAL DEFENSE:
SOME PEOPLE DO GET RAILROADED

O NE HALLOWEEN DAY, Scott, a finance executive, was working from home and eating lunch with his wife. He was wearing panties underneath his pants, in compliance with his wife's fetish; throughout their marriage she often asked him to wear women's undergarments. After lunch he left to run a quick errand at the pharmacy. Upon returning home to his country club estate, still clad in panties, he was greeted by a small army of local police in squad cars who placed him under arrest. He was accused of the felony abuse of his 12-year-old son, whom he allegedly had threatened at gunpoint against revealing to anyone his supposed extramarital affair. While handcuffed in the squad car, Scott, ever resourceful, managed to wriggle out of his feminine undies and stuff them in a pocket before being booked into county jail.

Scott had never been in trouble in his life. From a big family, he did well in high school. He became interested in business and graduated from the local state university. His ambition led him back east to a top business school. He married a fellow student he met in graduate school. Scott did everything right in life, except perhaps for his choice of the mother of his children.

If Scott were to plead to a lesser charge or get convicted on anything, he could kiss his career and kids goodbye. Concurrent with his criminal defense case was a family law and divorce case fighting for custody of his children. He hired a criminal defense lawyer, and the lawyer hired me to investigate on his behalf. We spent an intense four months working for him before the district attorney decided not to prosecute. His wife had apparently set him up that day of the police raid, having done her best at maneuvering to portray him as a panty-clad degenerate dad.

[86]

According to a police report and an emergency protective order, Scotty Jr. had made the allegations against his dad to a therapist. Scotty claimed he had seen dad with a mistress, Susie, jogging together several times and even on the side at a family vacation in Disneyland. The boy detailed how dad had pulled him aside one day at home, held a shotgun to his head, and warned him that if he told mom about Susie that he would hurt him, his sister, and mommy. In this session with the therapist, the boy also went into detail about how he didn't like going target shooting with his dad, how his dad was drunk all the time, and how much his dad's guns scared him. The police never bothered to check any of the information, simply taking the therapist's words and report at face value, and arrested Scott for several felonies. One of the local papers picked up the police blotter about Scott's arrest and published his name and the charge in print and on the Internet.

The police immediately should have spotted a credibility problem: Scotty Jr. was seeing the same therapist as his mother; as it turned out, the mother was steering her son's sessions. Obviously, the boy should have seen an independent professional. The marriage had its problems, but Scott swore that he had never been unfaithful to his wife or abusive to his two children. Perhaps at the root of the allegations was a play for Scott's assets. Scott had twice caught his wife spending almost $100,000 behind his back. He got so fed up with her wanton spending that he had a post-nuptial agreement drafted, which she signed, that separated their finances and established the two of them as separate financial entities. He did not want her destroying the family's credit and risking their financial livelihood.

My task was to go through each and every allegation contained in the therapist's report and the police report and blow them out of the water. Scott explained to us that likely his wife had coached his son and daughter to spy on his computer. He acknowledged to us that the alleged mistress was a former girlfriend from nearly 20 years ago. He supposed that his kids got her name, Susie, because he had exchanged a recent email with her and friended her on Facebook. Scott swore to us that the substance of the email included telling each other where they were in their respective relationships while acknowledging that trying to rekindle a romance would be impossible for so many factors. The kids likely

[87]

reported the Susie emails to their mother, who then became agitated and turned the kids against him.

When lies are specific enough in mentioning names, dates, places, and so on, they can be proven false. Susie gave email and other statements to me and later to police detectives that she had never been in California at the time when Scotty Jr. had supposedly seen her jogging with his dad or near the family in Disneyland; she had the timecards from her job to prove it. Scotty Jr. had alleged to the therapist that his dad drove drunk and was often drunk at home. But it was soon discovered that the children's definition of dad being "drunk" was having one beer. I went to all the restaurants the family frequented to interview waiters, waitresses, and management about Scott's drinking habits. Before these allegations surfaced, Scott had lost 20 or 30 pounds from reducing his already minimal alcohol intake as well as changing his eating habits. I learned from interviewing restaurant staff that Scott drank a lot of Diet Coke when out with his wife and kids. It's hard to lose that much weight if you are a heavy drinker.

Scotty Jr.'s claim that his dad had threatened him with a gun kept in one of the rooms, along with his own fear of guns, presented another fabrication to discredit (or shoot down?). Visits to local gun shops, gun ranges, and even the family's pastor established that Scotty Jr. genuinely liked being around guns, and even liked to target shoot .22 rifles with his dad. I found witnesses who knew that Scotty Jr. had never before seemed afraid of his dad, but worshipped him. Scott did keep weapons in the home, but they were always in a locked safe that neither the children nor anyone else other than Scott could access.

In sessions with an independent therapist, Scotty Jr. began giving more positive accounts about his dad. The independent monitor caught Scotty Jr. with a small tape recorder—apparently his mother was trying to secretly record their sessions. Concurrent with the criminal investigation was Scott's custody and divorce battle. Throughout the ordeal, Scott kept performing well at work, doing his best to be a good father while participating in his criminal defense.

The attorney and I had a couple of meetings with the police detective who had taken over the case. What's rare and commendable is that this detective listened to us. He wanted to get it right, but he never tipped his hand as to what he believed or whether he was taking a side. With Scott's direction, we put together a two-inch-thick binder of statement summaries, taped statements, and other evidence I had gathered. The detective said that he would talk with the district attorney assigned to the case.

Almost five months after his arrest, Scott's attorney learned that the district attorney would not be pursuing any charges against Scott. Scott got some measure of justice, but he still had to pay about $20,000 to the defense attorney and about $5,000 to me, just to clear his name.

Think about that for a bit. Do you imagine that poorer folks are never falsely arrested and accused of crimes? Scott had the resources to fight back, but what chance do low- or average-income people have? Last I heard, Scott is still duking it out in court over child custody and divorce.

Criminal defense cases are the most pulsating, focused, fundamental, and meaningful of all my work. Why? The stakes are highest. I am playing my part in the search for justice and dealing with core issues of fairness, liberty, constitutional rights, and all that other good stuff. If you can't rally to fight authority, then you are dead inside. On the line is the client's liberty, life, and reputation. I confess my biases. The police and the state have way, way too much power. Who makes up the pool of judges? I'm not sure but many come from the ranks of police and former prosecutors. About 80 percent of defendants can't afford private attorneys. My training as a reporter taught me to doubt authority; what stronger symbol of authority than the police? My disclaimer is that I like good cops and individual detectives. However, I see too many "true believers" in uniform who don't play fair and who lie in reports and testimony because they have gotten away with it for years. Why do people do anything? Because they can.

I have had close to 150 criminal defense investigations; many were through various conflicts or court-appointed programs where a local public defender was not available to take a case, so the court turns it over to a private attorney. The attorney then picks from a list of qualified private eyes. I see the reality of police work. It reminds me in many ways of deadline journalism in that it is geared to a narrow focus—i.e., make an arrest or get the story—and is often carried out in haste. There is of course a distinction between probable cause to make an arrest and whether a person is factually guilty. But back to the deadline journalism comparison: police in an urban environment work under time pressure and are subject to making honest mistakes. Their job is to arrest people. Sometimes, they might encounter witnesses who tell a different story. I have investigated more than a few cases where police talked to someone at a scene but didn't name potential witnesses in the report, or named them but did not take an accurate statement. I know, it's Monday-morning quarterbacking, but we are dealing with fundamental issues of human liberty and fairness.

Police are human and make mistakes. We as a society tend to give them way too much deference. They deserve respect, not blind loyalty. The most glaring oversight in detective work I have ever encountered happened in the course of an Oakland murder case several years ago. I read in the police report that the young male victim had been shot a couple times in a not-so-good part of town. Reading further I learned that police had found a scrap of paper with a woman's name and phone number on it. I believe this is called "a clue." This crime was by then several months old, but I called the woman's number. She answered and said that she had been with the victim earlier in the night. She told me that I was the first person to ask her about him and that police had never contacted her or spoken with her—maybe just because it was in Oakland, notorious for its severely overworked detective bureau. I don't think the oversight came up in the case, but the defendant was convicted.

Criminal defense work has also alerted me to the widespread use of boilerplate or cut-and-paste police reports. Drunk driving reports are notorious for standard police jargon. "I noticed slurred speech, watery eyes, and an unsteady gait," many DUI reports read. You also find catch-phrases in cases where police may have used too much force in making an arrest, to the point where the suspect is hospitalized with a concussion or maybe a few broken ribs. The reports all speak of "aggressive moves" by suspects leaving the officer no choice but to "neutralize the threat." For these and other reasons, I welcome the increasing use of body cameras on officers and dashcams in patrol cars. Such footage shows what police actually encounter in an arrest or stop situation and highlights the difficulty of their jobs. They are much braver men and women than I, but they should be held to the highest standard, equal to their power.

In all, criminal defense work has made me aware of the kind of manipulation police can engage in. There are all kinds of tricks and jockeying that go on in interview rooms, such as decisions about when a tape recorder gets turned on or off, whether police really stop questioning after a suspect asks for an attorney, whether the witness was promised something in exchange for testimony, the kind of bullying and brow-beating tactics police can use, the ways they can elicit false confessions, and so on. At the slightest hint that your interaction with police is not going well, be polite, be professional, and ask to speak with an attorney.

For these and other reasons, I enjoy working on criminal defense cases. I like battling Goliath. In criminal defense I have worked for Hell's Angels, business executives, and clients of just about all the major ethnic groups represented in the diverse state of California. The work reinforces my view that as private investigators we are really in the business of sales. If I can't sell someone on talking to me and cooperating or giving me a scrap of information, I will shortly be out of business when word gets around among attorneys that I'm not effective. My reputation cannot afford such a hit so I will keep selling.

A criminal defense attorney and his or her investigator usually has a fraction of the resources available to police and prosecutors. It's a stacked deck in favor of authority.

As we go to press I have a homicide defense case in San Jose where a young man, a college grad, stands accused of stabbing someone to death at a party at 3 a.m. in a drunken brawl. I should say I *had* a case, because the attorney I worked for became ill, resulting in the defendant getting a new attorney and investigator. He can't raise bail money, so he has been sitting in jail for more than six months. In his favor, no one saw him do the actual stabbing. It was a three-on-three fight between two groups and after it all broke up, the victim walked the 60 yards back to where the party was, and others noticed he was bleeding from the stomach. The victim had a .17 blood alcohol level and may have come at our client with a broken bottle. One of the many problems is that our client was too drunk to recall what occurred, but he did have a knife on him that night and at his apartment when he woke up. We lost our first big round in court when a judge ruled at the preliminary hearing that there was enough evidence to move forward to trial. As with many criminal defense cases, this one serves as a warning about what happens with alcohol in the wee hours.

My role in criminal defense investigations has not changed that much over the years. What I find interesting is that the public is becoming more skeptical of police and the judicial system. It seems that just about every day we read of another innocent man freed from prison and cleared of charges after new evidence comes forward. Among other shows, the popular podcast *Serial*, about a young Maryland man possibly wrongfully convicted in the murder of his girlfriend, serves to educate the public that not all police investigations are fair and that not every defendant gets good legal representation.

With the advent of more cameras in public, whether mounted on buildings, on smartphones, or in police body-worn devices, information and potential evidence keeps evolving and growing.

CHAPTER 15

THE FUTURE

PART I: TECHNOLOGY AND THE P.I.

AROUND THE TIME when Edward Snowden was first making news for releasing information about the National Security Agency's practices of gathering information on phone calls and electronic security monitoring, I attended a conference titled "Investigations for a Digital Age." The entire premise of the conference was that as investigators we'd better be up on the latest trends. Certainly, data mining and electronic evidence, whether on smartphones or computers, play an increasing role in investigations. What's the first thing police do at a scene when they question witnesses? They start going for cell phone information and will try to get what they can get from a phone. A recent Supreme Court ruling has said that police can seize the phone but can't inspect contents or the information that it contains without a search warrant. Electronic data has changed how police and lawyers investigate. I have to know about "stealth texting" applications or how to locate someone based on their tweets. I have read that 83 percent of people on Facebook have privacy settings set to "friends of friends", which can be exploited. I have recently taken webinars on social media and online background investigations.

I know enough to know what I don't know. In other words, if I am not conversant or do not know how something works, I will contract out to an investigator who does know electronic countermeasures for a "bug sweep" or knows how to inspect a computer for hidden files or web browser history. I need to keep up with technology advances, but I still believe more in the power of the investigator and overall investigation: it's the magician, not the wand.

At the "Digital Age" conference I was introduced to topics such as open source intelligence and updated on the latest fee-based databases available to private investigators. Facial recognition software is already available with certain computer applications and is only going to get bigger and bigger.

One P.I. who is also an attorney spoke at the conference about businesses specializing in electronic discovery. As he puts it: "Eighty-nine percent of evidence these days is electronic." His company sifts through all the electronic data in the discovery process of lawsuits. Of that electronic evidence, 90 percent is emails.

As I sat there in Silicon Valley with my colleagues, I experienced a sort of tech inferiority complex. I started to feel a bit better because as tech experts discover more names and places and dates, lawsuits will fly and more people will have to be found and subpoenaed—all of which should result in even more business for me. Technology is merely a tool, a most wondrous shortcut that includes GPS and Internet aggregators.

After the conference, one of my database providers started offering license plate reader data for sale. The database provider has sources who sell this information to them. The database pulls information from license plate readers operated by police, mall security vehicles, and commercial parking lots, or simply positioned along random streets and highways. The data can include the location of the vehicle, the plate number, and maybe even an image of the driver or a passenger. Maybe it can be used to see whose car is at the medical marijuana dispensary or near a Planned Parenthood or parked at the bar at 2 a.m.

I tested this new database license plate reader out on myself. Guess where I saw images of my car and its license plate? In the parking garage at the "Digital Age" conference in Santa Clara! Part of me is creeped out by such tech-based tools, but the other part knows that they represent merely the latest progression in how we gather information. As a society we gather data and disseminate it at faster and faster speeds. In defense of the database provider, they are merely spreading and selling information that is already in the public eye, the difference being that it's historical and can be accessed indefinitely. Technology is outpacing legislative attempts to deal with it—it's ahead of society deciding what the rules should be.

It's strange to notice how one day I'm at a conference hearing about the latest technologies and then the next day, or year, I'm using the technology in an investigation and even testifying about it.

A few years ago, I had a family law matter in which I was working for a grandmother trying to get visitation rights with her six-year-old grandson. At issue in the case was whether her son actually lived with his wife. The son and his wife had testified that they were still together as a couple. The grandmother told me that her son, who has a felony conviction to his name, was a big-time pot dealer who lived at various marijuana grow houses. If it could be shown that they were not living together, then the grandmother would gain visitation rights.

Dopers are notoriously difficult to follow. They are quick to sniff out any tail or surveillance. I knew the license plate number of the son and ran it though the license plate reader. Sure enough, his car showed up as being parked numerous times late at night and early in the morning at an address other than what he testified to in his deposition. My associate Al and I now had a place to watch. But in the meantime he had changed his cars again. In the week before the trial started, he rather obviously started leaving his new car parked at the apartment where he claimed to live with his wife. I now had another license plate to run. The plate reader showed the new car visiting the suspected grow house late at night as well as being parked at his apartment.

In the first few days of trial, in front of a judge rather than a jury, I testified about my direct observations of where I had seen his cars as well as on what the license plate reader data showed. Opposing counsel vehemently objected to the license plate reader. "No, he is an expert and I want to hear about it," the judge said. I smiled on the inside. I testified that the database company shared with me how the data is collected. The opposing counsel had me admit that I did not know specifically who had taken the photos used in the plate reader data.

But the biggest evidentiary nugget from the plate readers was it gave me an address that lead to my finding the landlords to subpoena. I tracked them down in San Jose. The landlord testified that the son had paid rent on the house for the last two years. The landlord also brought the copies of the cashier's checks from the son and the text messages he had exchanged with him. I had poked a huge hole in the son's credibility. He switched from denying in depositions and in trial that he had ever lived apart from his wife to his attorney putting him back on the stand with an improbable story that he was paying rent for other people at the house. He also testified that he rented the house as a place to grow medical marijuana solely for his own consumption.

Guess what? We lost at trial. Despite my testimony and that of the landlord, the judge ruled that the evidence wasn't strong enough. The client, her attorney, and I were floored. The judge believed the convicted felon and pot dealer. Losing is never easy and the client and the attorney had a lot more at stake than I had. The attorney appealed but the judge denied his arguments.

New technology will keep working its way through the legal and justice systems like vines attaching to a fence. Investigators will still find use for the traditional skills of interviewing witnesses and documenting evidence, but technology is quickly changing the nature of our job.

Certain private investigators exploit the new tech and social media investigation angles. They are smart to see that attorneys and the public don't know that much about certain technologies such as cell phones. If they are good at it and providing a needed service and delivering results for clients, more power to them. In the same way, I leverage my knowledge of public records and the intricacies of obtaining information from California courts and government.

There is always a bit of snake oil hucksterism in my industry. About eight years ago I started noticing private investigator websites with pictures of big world maps and dancing computer screens with lightning bolts shooting out of them. Their choice of web design was intended to suggest that they could procure information worldwide just by pressing a few buttons on the computer. Presto! These private investigators are reinforcing what is known as the CSI Effect, an exaggerated portrayal by TV shows of how forensic and digital evidence really works. The public that watches these shows, such as *The Good Wife*, and expects a certain amount of evidentiary razzle-dazzle, is the same public that sits on juries. Maybe you've seen the episodes where the in-house law firm investigator or hotshot cop hacks into a computer and can somehow zoom a remote camera to reveal a full and clear license plate from a mile away.

I've seen the elephant and heard the owl when it comes to fads and gimmicks that cycle through the industry every few years.

Last year the private investigator app "Trustify" launched. It was first called "Flimflam," a more apt name for the dubious service on offer. The founder, not a licensed P.I., started the company after he felt he had been ripped off by paying a private investigator $1,500 in a divorce case of his in Northern Virginia and not getting results. The concept is that for a low hourly fee people can use the app to hire a private investigator. However, the fee is shared with the app and the private investigator makes about $35 an hour. (Fast and cheap will never be quality.) I doubt professional private investigators in an urban area will accept working for $35 an hour. Furthermore, there are questions about how the app vets the P.I. or whether the app or the P.I. bears the responsibility if the client turns out to be a stalker. Few of my professional colleagues consider the app, a self-proclaimed Uber for private investigations, as a serious competitor to our services. It could work better if the investigator and client screening procedures were tightened and the hourly pay for the P.I. were increased.

A local private investigator providing excellent service will always be in demand. Consumers can always cut corners and save on costs. But a phone interview is never as good as seeing someone in person, observing body language, and sizing them up as credible or unreliable. No amount of monitoring someone's social media feeds will tell you about their real activities or replace boots-on-the ground surveillance. Do people post status updates such as "Psyched for nooner with the mistress" or "Going to Mexico on vacation and to launder money"?

Twenty years ago, I was quoted in an article in the *San Francisco Chronicle*. The article's thesis was that the Internet would hurt private investigators who make a living from skip tracing, that is, finding people. I told the reporter that the prediction was wrong. I was right then and I'm right now.

Technology without the human element is just as flat as an interview devoid of facts to check. Private investigators will always play a part in digesting the information, which for all its new ways of being gathered still needs to be sifted, vetted, and verified.

THE FUTURE, PART II: WHAT I'VE LEARNED

Speaking of the human element, it's time I asked: how have job and my daily routine affected me as a person? Has it warped my soul? Do I look under my bed at night, GPS my wife's car, and track the dog's every movement with covert cameras? Overall, I think I keep my suspicious side contained and maintain a healthy barrier between Mike the Investigator and Mike the Dude. I don't do background checks on my neighbors, and I trust most strangers. I have a reserved personality, but I still like people.

On the practical side, a career as a private investigator has made me aware of how dangerous certain situations can be, for example walking without using a crosswalk or not having good lighting on a bicycle at night. If not on a surveillance, I tend to drive the standard five miles per hour over the speed limit.

I have seen horrible situations, such as the aftermaths of shooting deaths and traffic collisions. But even in those dark moments a surprising amount of kindness will occur. Complete strangers will offer comfort to people bleeding in the street. They hold their hand or try to keep them calm and warm until medical help arrives. The Good Samaritans are distinct from the paid first responders. They jump in to help without any obligation.

In the domestic cases I've come to realize that most clients already know that their partner is cheating—what they are looking for is absolute proof to help make a decision. And yes, making money off others' misfortunes does not necessarily feel good, but obtaining evidence or proof that helps a client make a decision is rewarding. I help people move forward in their lives.

As I age I find I am more protective of people. I go out of my way to get results in the elder abuse and fraud cases. Helping victims of any crime is its own reward. Looking at the ledger of whether the job has impressed me or depressed me about the human condition, I would have to say I am slightly impressed. As long as people are mean and have bad judgment, I have some measure of job security.

A few changes at my business are underway. I have hired part-time workers on payroll, as opposed to my old way of only using independent contractors. First, there was Josh, who did court-appointed criminal cases. I had planned to train him to handle all the ordinary tasks so that I could focus on the big cases and on growing the business. But Josh has moved to Portland, Oregon. I have just replaced him with Angela, a former journalist who is also a paralegal. It feels good to mentor employees in the way John Nazarian mentored me. I have a payroll to meet and would like to add another one or two part-time workers. Working with new employees brings welcomed new energy to my business.

The partnership with Elrod will be coming to an end as he has moved to Nevada where he has a business making custom rifles. My wife and I sold our house in Oakland to move to Fremont, about 25 miles south, so that she could be closer to her work just outside of San Jose. (A three-hour round-trip commute in the congested Bay Area makes for a cranky spouse.)

The beautiful dog on the front and back of this book, Daisy, died of cancer in January 2017. She will be forever missed. I'm now training a yellow female lab puppy, Buttercup.

I might only have another 15 years of good work in me, so I have to be smart about the path I chart. To that end, I'm moving more into management. I will be the one coordinating the cases and surveillance if not always conducting the fieldwork.

At this point I'm professionally obligated to close with a Dashiell Hammett quote about being a private investigator in the San Francisco Bay Area. I can't think of anything pithier than that old-school observation that as a P.I., you are either a hero or a bum.

Am I happy? At times, yes. Some days I wish I was a hotshot investigative journalist in a rumpled but expensive suit, maybe appearing on public television news panels to utter "if you will" while stroking my goatee. I don't believe in permanent happiness. The satisfaction of my work comes from the process of what it takes to obtain information and to win the case, helping private clients and attorneys, and playing a part in the broader judicial system.

As a P.I., I don't have a grand pronouncement or ultimate advice, other than to trust your gut and watch out for each other.